The impact of t

Kojo Amissah

The impact of the self-fulfilling prophecy on Black Deaf male students

Roxy -
The reminder that life's challenges are not forever.
Thanks.
Dr. K.

Scholar's Press

Impressum / Imprint

Bibliografische Information der Deutschen Nationalbibliothek: Die Deutsche Nationalbibliothek verzeichnet diese Publikation in der Deutschen Nationalbibliografie; detaillierte bibliografische Daten sind im Internet über http://dnb.d-nb.de abrufbar.
Alle in diesem Buch genannten Marken und Produktnamen unterliegen warenzeichen-, marken- oder patentrechtlichem Schutz bzw. sind Warenzeichen oder eingetragene Warenzeichen der jeweiligen Inhaber. Die Wiedergabe von Marken, Produktnamen, Gebrauchsnamen, Handelsnamen, Warenbezeichnungen u.s.w. in diesem Werk berechtigt auch ohne besondere Kennzeichnung nicht zu der Annahme, dass solche Namen im Sinne der Warenzeichen- und Markenschutzgesetzgebung als frei zu betrachten wären und daher von jedermann benutzt werden dürften.

Bibliographic information published by the Deutsche Nationalbibliothek: The Deutsche Nationalbibliothek lists this publication in the Deutsche Nationalbibliografie; detailed bibliographic data are available in the Internet at http://dnb.d-nb.de.
Any brand names and product names mentioned in this book are subject to trademark, brand or patent protection and are trademarks or registered trademarks of their respective holders. The use of brand names, product names, common names, trade names, product descriptions etc. even without a particular marking in this work is in no way to be construed to mean that such names may be regarded as unrestricted in respect of trademark and brand protection legislation and could thus be used by anyone.

Coverbild / Cover image: www.ingimage.com

Verlag / Publisher:
Scholar's Press
ist ein Imprint der / is a trademark of
OmniScriptum GmbH & Co. KG
Heinrich-Böcking-Str. 6-8, 66121 Saarbrücken, Deutschland / Germany
Email: info@scholars-press.com

Herstellung: siehe letzte Seite /
Printed at: see last page
ISBN: 978-3-639-70897-4

Zugl. / Approved by: Phoenix, University of Phoenix Online, Dissertation 2013

Copyright © 2015 OmniScriptum GmbH & Co. KG
Alle Rechte vorbehalten. / All rights reserved. Saarbrücken 2015

ABSTRACT

This qualitative descriptive study purposed to explore the perceptions of a purposive sample of 20 Black Deaf male students and alumni in postsecondary in Washington, District of Columbia to determine if the self-fulfilling prophecy theory contributed to their pedagogy. A qualitative survey was administered and the data was analyzed with Excel. Fifteen self-fulfilling prophecy themes emerged from the analysis: (a) syllabic expectations, (b) self expectations, (c) no-low-high expectations, (d) eye contact-acknowledgement, (e) attitudinal indifference, (f) public praise-positive-negative comments, (g) personalized one-on-one attention, (h) pop quiz reminders, (i) office hours-after class counseling, (j) team assignments, (k) verbal-written-positive-negative feedback, (l) private-public-verbal-written reinforcements, (m) probing, (n) reminders, and (o) self-motivation. The results indicated that Black Deaf male students and alumni perception about their educational experience in the classroom were positive, Galatea effects.

DEDICATION

I am externally grateful for support from my father, my mother, my sister, my brothers, my son, and my daughter. I love you all. I want to thank them for believing in me.

ACKNOLEDGMENTS

I thank and acknowledge committee members Dr. Janice Monroe and Dr. Richard Bothel for their patience, support, and insightful suggestions. I especially thank my mentor, Dr. Julia Bao, for her patience, guidance, persistence to complete this dissertation, and encouragement. A special thank you to Dr. Roberto Davila, 10th President of Gallaudet University, I would not have began this journey without your appointment, guidance, and for giving me a chance. I acknowledge my dissertation support team members Dr. Mary Keane and Mr. Gabriel Fischer for continued support and for being a constant reminder that we can do it! I acknowledge my editor, Ms. Trudy Suggs of T.S. Writing Services, LLC, for her amazing editing skills. I acknowledge my sign language interpreters, Mrs. Danita L. Brooks and Mr. Larry Kenneybrew, for their outstanding interpretation during my residencies. I finally acknowledge the support of my sister Mrs. Milady Simpson for being the backbone I needed at times when I almost gave up. Your support and belief in me from the start of this journey is truly appreciated. Stay blessed.

TABLE OF CONTENTS

List of Tables xii

Chapter 1: Introduction 1

    Background of the Problem 2

    Statement of the Problem 3

    Purpose of the Study 4

    Significance of the Study 5

    Nature of the Study 6

        Research method 6

        Research design 8

    Research Questions 9

    Theoretical Framework 11

    Definition of Terms 14

    Assumptions 15

    Scope, Limitations, and Delimitations 16

        Scope 16

        Limitations 16

        Delimitations 16

    Summary 17

Chapter 2: Review of the Literature 18

    Documentation and Literature on the SFP theory 18

    Literature Review 19

        Historical Overview 19

    The self-fulfilling prophecy 21

Current Findings 29

The Self-Fulfilling Prophecy and Academic Achievement 32

    The self-fulfilling prophecy and learning 35

    The self-fulfilling prophecy and life choices 41

History of Deaf and Hard of Hearing Black males 45

    Dualism of culture and identity development – Deaf and Black 50

    Psychology and identity development 51

    Black and Deaf 52

    Sociology and identity development 53

    Social psychology and identity development 54

    Human and developmental ecology and identity development 55

Gaps in the Literature 59

Summary 59

Chapter 3: Method 61

Research Method and Design Appropriateness 61

Population 64

Sample Frame 65

Informed Consent 65

Confidentiality 66

Geographic Location 66

Instrumentation 66

Data Collection 67

Pilot Study	67
Validity	68
Internal validity	68
External validity	68
Data Analysis	68
Procedures	69
Content analysis	69
Coding	70
Coding process	70
Summary	72
Chapter 4: Analysis and Results	74
Pilot Study	75
Data Collection	75
Demographics	77
Presentation of data analysis	77
Findings	79
Themes	80
Syllabic expectations	81
Self-expectation	83
No/low/high/unclear expectations	83
Eye contact/acknowledgment	84
Attitudinal indifference	85
Public praise – positive/negative comments	86

- Personalized one-on-one attention 86
- Pop-quiz reminders 87
- Office hours/after class counseling 87
- Team assignments 88
- Verbal/written – positive/negative feedback 88
- Private/public – verbal/written reinforcements 89
- Probing 90
- Reminders 90
- Self motivation 90

Summary 91

Chapter 5: Conclusions and Recommendations 92

Research Findings 92
- Response rate 92
- Interpretation 93
- Implications 93

Emergent Themes 94
- Theme 1: Syllabic expectations 95
- Theme 2: Self-expectations 95
- Theme 3: No/high/low/expectations 96
- Theme 4: Eye contact/acknowledgement 97
- Theme 5: Attitudinal indifference 98
- Theme 6: Public praise – positive/negative comments 99
- Theme 7: Personalized one-on-one attention 100

        Themes 8 and 9: Pop quiz reminders and office hours after class

            counseling 102

        Theme 10: Team assignments 103

        Theme 11: Verbal/written – positive/negative-feedback 104

        Theme 12: Private/public – verbal/written reinforcements 105

        Theme 13: Probing 106

        Theme 14: Reminders 106

        Theme 15: Self-motivation 107

    Limitations 108

    Recommendations 109

        Recommendation for Black Deaf male students 109

        Recommendation for faculty 110

        Recommendation for higher education leaders 111

        Recommendation for future research 112

    Significance to Leadership 113

    Conclusion 114

References 117

Appendix A: Informed Consent Form 137

Appendix B: Survey Questions 138

Appendix C: Collaboration Letter 147

Appendix D: Payment Form 148

Appendix E: Recruitment Poster 149

Appendix F: Invitation Letter 150

Appendix G: Alumni Recruitment Email Advertisement 151

Appendix H: Tables 152

LIST OF TABLES

Table 1 *Educational Theories and Implications* 25

Table 2 *Golem and Galatea effects, and Differential Treatments* 28

Table 3 *Five SFP steps, Five Race, Class, and Achievement Realities and Implications*. 34

Table 4 *The Four-Factor Theory and Implications for Learning* 37

Table 5 *Five SFP steps and Role Model Behaviors* 44

Table 6 *Chronological History of Deaf Individuals* 47

Table 7 *Cultural Dualism and Identity Development* 58

Table 8 *Sample content analysis* 72

Table 9 *Emergent Themes and Textual Description* 80

Table 10 *Formed Expectations Themes* 81

Table 11 *Differential Treatment Themes* 84

Table 12 *Modes of Communication Themes* 87

Table 13 *Consistency Themes* 88

Table 14 *SFP Themes* 89

Table 15 *Teacher Forms Expectation Questions* 152

Table 16 *Differential Manner Questions* 152

Table 17 *Behaviors and Achievement Questions* 153

Table 18 *Consistency Treatment Questions* 153

Table 19 *Conform to Expectations Questions* 154

Table 20 *Teacher Expectations Participants* 155

Table 20a *Illuminations: Teacher Expectations* 156

Table 21 *Positive Expectations Participants* 157

Table 21a *Annotations: Positive Expectations* 158

Table 22 *Negative Expectations Participants* 159

Table 22a *Elucidations: Negative Expectations* 160

Table 23 *Statistics: Teacher Expectations* 161

Table 24 *Differential Treatment Participants* 162

Table 24a *Rationalizations: Perception of Expectations* 163

Table 25 *Communication of Expectations Participants* 164

Table 25a *Undertones: Communication of Expectation* 165

Table 26 *Classroom Learning Participants* 166

Table 26a *Observations: Classroom Learning* 167

Table 27 *Data: Differential Treatment* 168

Table 28 *Behavior and Achievement Participants* 169

Table 28a *Commentaries: Discouraging Feedback* 170

Table 29 *Defied Expectations Participants* 171

Table 29a *Annotations: Defied Expectations* 172

Table 30 *Records: Behavior and Achievement* 173

Table 31 *Consistent Treatment Participants* 174

Table 31a *Testimonies: Encouraged Feedback* 175

Table 32 *Helpful Activities Participants* 176

Table 32a *Inquiries: Success Activities* 177

Table 33 *Performed Above Expectations Participants* 178

Table 33a *Accounts: Exceeded Expectations* 179

Table 34 *Outperformed Classmates Participants* 180

Table 34a *Enquiries: Excelled Performance* 181

Table 35 *Indicators: Consistent Treatment* 182

Table 36 *Conform to the SFP Participants* 183

Table 36a *Mentions: Academically Challenged* 184

Table 37 *Failed due to Expectations* 185

Table 37a *Inquests: Academic Failure due to Expectations* 186

Table 38 *Succeeded due to Expectations* 187

Table 38a *Interpositions: Academic Success due to Expectations* 188

Table 39 *Figures: SFP* 189

Chapter 1

Introduction

The self-fulfilling prophecy (SFP) phenomenon is "a *false* definition [*a priori*] of the situation evoking a new behavior [*a posteriori*], which makes the original false conception come *true*" (Merton, 1948, p. 195). Rubie-Davies, Hattie, and Hamilton (2006) identified the Golem effect – a negative expectation [*a priori*] sustained by differential treatment [*a posteriori*], and the Galatea effect – a positive expectation [*a priori*] enhanced by differential treatment [*a posteriori*] within the SFP literature. Minorities were overrepresented as a Golem-effect population within special education programs (Baglieri & Moses, 2010; Rubie-Davies et al., 2006).

However, the literature was ambiguous about the cultural and ethnicity implications on the Black Deaf male student, a Golem-effect population's pedagogic experiences and low achievement (Guyll, Madon, Prieto, & Scherr, 2010; McCaskill, 2005). Academic achievement was an important social concern because the functionalist theorists hypothesized that education was a navigational compass to social advancement and status (Beaver, 2009). This SFP phenomenon exploration focused on two major areas: theoretical study on didactic interactions and *a priori* expectations, and sustained *a posteriori* differential treatment and its impact in higher education.

Research in these areas provided profound knowledge in the SFP field. The qualitative descriptive research findings highlighted the cultural dualism complexity and academic needs of Black Deaf male students. There was a deliberate emphasis to generate awareness to educate advocates, policymakers, leadership, educational leadership, and teachers.

Background of the Problem

The influence of SFP on the achievements of minority students was a widely discussed problem in relevant literature (Al-Fadhi & Singh, 2006; Couch, 2010; Hinnant, O'Brien, & Ghazarian, 2009; Merton, 1948; Rosenthal & Jacobson, 1968; Tauber, 1997; Tsiplakides & Keramida, 2010; Wong & Hui, 2006). The challenge was that minorities consisted of Blacks, Asians, Hispanics, and individuals with disabilities. Each minority category was multifaceted by cultural, ethnic, and sub-group complexities that were generalized in the SFP research.

Black Deaf males were a minority sub-group embedded within the Black hearing males and disabilities populations (Guyll et al., 2010; McCaskill, 2005). This population was overrepresented as a Golem-effect group in special education programs with little understanding of their culture dualism and ethnic complex educational needs (Baglieri & Moses, 2010; Guyll et al., 2010; McCaskill, 2005; Rubie-Davies et al., 2006). The overrepresentation of Black Deaf male students in special education was SFP, and caused this population to fall through the cracks in the achievement data discussion (Sears, 2008; U.S. Department of Education, 2007, 2010). The underlying message was a negative expectation, *a priori* made evident by the differential treatment of questionable national education reports, *a posteriori* (Sears, 2008; U.S. Department of Education, 2007, 2010).

Guyll et al. (2010) found a linkage between "educational outcomes, SFP, stigma consciousness, and stereotype threat processes" (p. 126). Therefore, a Black Deaf male who identified with Black culture experienced Golem effects and overrepresentation in special education programs (Baglieri & Moses, 2010; Green, 2005; Rubie-Davies et al., 2006). A Black Deaf male who identified with Deaf culture experienced Deaf and disability Golem effects and faced a possibility of intellectual disability misdiagnosis (Skiba et al., 2008). The implications of the cultural dualism perspective were not specified in governmental and research reports (Guyll et al., 2010; U.S. Department of Education, 2007, 2010).

Implicit government and research reports led faculty and educational leaders to presume that Black Deaf male students and special education students shared similar educational obstacles (Harper & Nichols, 2008). However, Harper and Nichols (2008) warned that "an enormous assumption is often made that Black men, one of the most stereotyped groups on college and university campuses, all share common experiences and backgrounds" (p. 199). Such assumptions were foundations of the SFP theory and research, which aligned with the functionalist, and symbolic interactionist educational theories (Beaver, 2009; Crossley, 2010; Smit & Fritz, 2008).

Stereotyped assumptions were theoretical concerns to the SFP research and the functionalist theory (Harper & Nichols, 2008). This theory postulated that higher education knowledge and skills created a navigational compass to social advancement and status (Beaver, 2009). The symbolic interactionist theorists analyzed educational interaction in the classroom environment for equitable knowledge and skills development (Smit & Fritz, 2008). The two theories were critical to this research problem because individuals and groups used education as a social advancement ticket to gain and retain status (Breen, 2010).

Statement of the Problem

The general problem was that Black Deaf male students experienced Black and Deaf cultural dualism, ethnicity challenges, and overrepresentation in special education programs. These experiences were susceptible to the self-fulfilling prophecy phenomena and low graduation rates (Green, 2005; Guyll et al., 2010; McCaskill, 2005). The specific problem was that the Black Deaf male student's perception of teacher expectations about his academic abilities and the teacher's expectations were influencing his overall academic achievement. This qualitative descriptive purposive sampling study surveyed Black Deaf male students and alumni to explore their perceptions of their educational experience in the postsecondary setting (Neuman, 2006). The intent of the investigation was to understand the SFP influence on this population's achievement or underachievement.

Purpose of the Study

The purpose of this qualitative descriptive study was to explore the perceptions of a purposive sample of Black Deaf male students in postsecondary setting in Washington, D.C. to determine if the SFP theory contributed to their pedagogic achievements. A qualitative descriptive method was appropriate for this type of inquiry to explain the perceptions of this study population classroom experience (Creswell, 2005). A critical sample size of Black Deaf males at a postsecondary setting in Washington, D.C., were chosen for this study because this population had the lowest postsecondary graduation rates among minority students (Creswell, 2005; Gallaudet University Enrollment Reports 2000-2006; JBHE, 2007; U.S. Department of Education, 2009).

According to Neuman (2006), descriptive research design allows the researcher to explore the in-depth perceptions of the targeted population. A descriptive research design was appropriate to look beyond statistical explanations to theories by exploring additional multiple external factors (Creswell, 2005). The data was analyzed for emerging themes and patterns of SFP using Microsoft Excel software. The research outcomes might highlight coping strategies in postsecondary setting for Black Deaf male students. The outcomes also could create awareness among educational leadership about how to improve statistical data reporting systems, faculty development training programs, and new policies to enhance minority student retention in postsecondary setting.

Significance of the Problem

Higher education knowledge and skills were a navigational compass to social advancement and status (Breen, 2010). Drucker (1999) added, "the most valuable asset of a 21st century institution (whether business or non-business) will be its *knowledge workers* and their *productivity*" (p. 79). However, scholarly discourse about educational attainment and academic achievement during pre- and post-*Brown* v. *Board of Education* failed to discuss the Black Deaf male student's academic experience (McCaskill, 2005). Salend and Garrick Dunhaney (2005), added higher education practitioners needed to examine the multiple factors that contributed to the disproportionate representation of students of color in special education programs. Disadvantaged student dropout rates affected higher education funding patterns, facilities planning, and the labor market because disadvantaged students were unprepared for the responsibilities associated with vocations (Roessler & Foshee, 2010).

This disquisition appended knowledge to the SFP research and its influence on the academic performance and achievement of individuals with disabilities, specifically focusing on the Black Deaf male students. This research subjoined knowledge to the functionalist and symbolic interactionist theories (Beaver, 2009; Smit & Fritz, 2008), which heightened leadership awareness to segregate achievement reports about minorities and individuals with disabilities. This inquiry was important to educational leaders, advocates, and policy makers. They used the outcomes of the study to make critical decisions about the educational needs of minority students, retention of minority students, and improve statistical data reporting systems. The corollaries illustrated some of the factors that influence Black Deaf male students' academic performance.

Nature of the Study

Research method. The study used a qualitative descriptive method to explain and understand the perceptions of the Black Deaf male classroom experience in a postsecondary setting (Creswell, 2005). The research utilized a qualitative research method because it was an emerging process that evolves the research purpose and questions to understand participant feedback (Creswell, 2005). The evolution process "expands the researcher's knowledge about the study from the participants" (Creswell, 2005, p. 132).

In contrast to qualitative research designs, several researchers (Creswell, 2005; Hrabowski III et al., 1998; Neuman, 2006) speculated that a quantitative research approach failed to expose misconceptions about disadvantaged groups. Neuman (2006) added that qualitative research was different from a case study in that a researcher focused on several factors or compared a limited set of cases. Also, quantitative and mixed-methods research designs incorporated hypothesis, theories, and variables, that were mathematically driven (Creswell, 2005). Creswell (2005) further stated, "Quantitative research is deductive, and research questions and hypothesis do not change during the study" (p. 133).

The purpose of this study was to explore the perceptions of Black Deaf male students and alumni classroom experience to determine if the SFP theory contributed to their pedagogic achievements. The research examined Black Deaf male postsecondary students and alumni in Washington, D.C. who graduated with a grade point average between 2.0 and 4.0. The goal was to understand the descriptive relationship of the SFP and achievements on this population.

A qualitative research method was appropriate for this study because it sought to provide detailed interpretations and meanings of factors that could be causing the low graduation rates of Black Deaf male students and alumni (Hjelmeland & Knizek, 2010). This method was proper for this inquiry because this population's low graduation rate was quantified with little understanding about the causes (Williamson, 2007). This approach provided an in-depth understanding of how multiple external forces guided the research design.

A quantitative method was not appropriate for this probe. Meadows-Orlans (2001) found that it was difficult to obtain statistical samples because this research population was a low-incidence population. The quantitative methodology was not proper for this disquisition because the focus was to understand each individual's perspective and expectations of his academic experience beyond the mathematical interpretations (Hoy, 2009). The mathematical approach provided an understanding of how often a phenomenon occurred and the qualitative explored what caused the phenomenon (Castellan, 2010).

"Mixed method designs are procedures for collecting, analyzing, and linking both quantitative and qualitative data in a single study or in multiphase series of studies"

(Creswell, 2005, p. 53). The mixed method did not fit the goal of this inquiry. The intent of this probe was to understand the deep-seated reasons that caused the low achievement of Black Deaf male students.

Research design. The purpose of this research was to look beyond statistical explanations to theories by exploring additional multiple external factors about the perceptions of the study population classroom experience (Creswell, 2005). The descriptive approach became visible to researchers in the early 20th century (Morgan, 2007). Since that time, several researchers advocated its viability (Campbell & Roden, 2010; Creswell, 2005; Germain & Quinn, 2005; Fortune & Gillespie, 2010). The descriptive design concentrated on the perceptions of the participants beyond the simple logic of quantitative research. Descriptive study offered interpretations to the complex experiences that eluded quantitative research.

According to Campbell and Roden (2010), grounded research theory design was not concerned with the explanation of culture or experience. The grounded theories design "explains an educational process of events, activities, actions, and interactions that occur over time" (Creswell, 2005, p. 396). In contrast, an ethnographic research approach offered the researcher an opportunity to participate in the research, which may not be appropriate for this inquiry (Campbell & Roden, 2010).

The qualitative descriptive design was appropriate for this research. The aim was to explore the *a posteriori* differential treatment perceptions of the study population's pedagogic experience. Another aim was to understand their culturally dualistic experiences.

Creswell (2005) defined research designs as the "procedures for collecting, analyzing, and reporting research in quantitative and qualitative research" (p. 281). This probe employed a qualitative open-ended survey instrument. The instrument was administered to Black Deaf male undergraduate students attending school and Black Deaf male alumni.

The intent of this inquisition to determine how the SFP theory was contributing and contributed to their scholastic outcomes. The open-ended survey was pilot-tested by five undergraduate Black Deaf male students who attended the selected research site in Washington, D.C. The pilot-tested undergraduates were excluded from the study to validate the survey instrument and process.

The open-ended survey was administered to undergraduate subjects and sent via the United States Postal Service to alumni subjects to obtain descriptive data, which were analyzed using Microsoft Excel software. The data were analyzed for SFP themes such as teacher expectations, differential treatment, behavior and achievement verbalization, achievement consistency, and time (Merton, 1948; Tauber, 1997). The open-ended survey questions revealed the opinions and perceptions of the SFP phenomena among the study population.

Research Questions

This qualitative descriptive study used open-ended survey questions to investigate the influence of the SFP phenomenon on the Black Deaf male student. This study anticipated revealing the culturally dualistic experiences of the Black Deaf male student in postsecondary setting. This research allowed participants to note experiences during didactic interactions inside the classroom in postsecondary environment to identify SFP themes. The two research questions were: (R1) how do Black Deaf male students perceive a teacher's expectations of their academic performances in postsecondary institutions, and (R2) how do Black Deaf male students perceive teacher expectations influence on their achievements?

The first question investigated perceived SFP themes as factors that influenced the Black Deaf male student's academic performance in postsecondary. The second question explored perceived teacher expectations that influenced their academic achievements. Investigating the perceptions of Black Deaf male students in the postsecondary setting uncovered coping strategies for this population, professional development topics for faculty, mentorship, and to begin a new research discourse about the study population. This study outcome was projected to assist policy makers to consider modifications in the achievement report systems to reveal Black Deaf male students' pedagogic experiences.

The Black Deaf male student's academic experience was scarcely noted in research data (Meadow-Orlans, 2001). Lack of data challenged researchers to isolate specific reasons for low graduation rates and achievements of this population (Gallaudet University Enrollment Reports, 2008). Researchers argued the SFP phenomenon was one of the factors that influenced the academic experiences of minorities and individuals with disabilities (Hinnant et al., 2009; Rosenthal & Jacobson, 1968; Rubie-Davies et al., 2006). Researchers also hypothesized that teacher *a priori* negative, or positive expectations originated the SFP influences that affect *a posteriori* pedagogic achievement.

Theoretical Framework

This qualitative descriptive research study explored the *a posteriori* perception of the Black Deaf male student in a postsecondary setting. The literature on Deaf and hard of hearing postsecondary experiences categorized the Black Deaf male population under generic and inclusive labels (Green, 2005; Mehra, Eavey, & Keamy, 2009; Richardson, Marschark, Sarchet, & Sapere, 2010; U.S. Department of Education, 2007, 2010). Some of the commonly known labels were special education, mentally retarded, children with hearing loss, Deaf and hard of hearing, and children with hearing impairment (Green, 2005; Mehra et al., 2009; Richardson et al., 2010; U.S. Department of Education, 2007, 2010). Sufficient research was unavailable that focused on postsecondary achievements of American Black Deaf male students.

The theoretical framework of this qualitative descriptive study compared with other SFP research (Hinnant et al., 2009 Merton, 1948; Rosenthal & Jacobson, 1968; Tauber, 1997). These researchers concluded that the SFP phenomenon influenced the academic achievement of individuals with disabilities, a minority subgroup. The literature was indistinguishable about the SFP phenomenon relationship to Black Deaf male students, a minority subgroup's academic achievement.

The Black Deaf male was typically generalized as a minority, individual with disability, Deaf and hard of hearing, special education, mentally retarded, and disability in the literature (U.S. Department of Education, 2007, 2010). Harper and Nichols (2008) concluded that each minority category, especially Black males, did not have the same academic needs. Therefore, the generic categorization framework, while a standard practice at the U.S. Department of Education, (2007, 2010) was SFP *a priori* Golem effects.

The Golem effects were negative *a priori* expectations that impede student achievement (Rubie-Davies et al., 2006). The generic categorization intentional or not subtly sent the Golem effects message that this study population achievement was insignificant. The insignificant perspective was another example of negative teacher expectation stereotype (Harper & Nichols, 2008; Hinnant et al., 2009).

Teacher expectations research were based on stereotypes and preconceived notions that the Black Deaf male, assumed to function like the Black hearing male, could not succeed academically (Harper & Nichols, 2008; Hinnant et al., 2009). The literature disconfirmed that a Black Deaf male experienced a different kind of stereotype because deafness was a hidden disability. A hidden disability might have prompted teachers and educators to assume that a Black Deaf male student was hearing until he identified himself as otherwise (Mackenzie & Smith, 2009).

Harper and Nichols (2008) concluded that undergraduate Black males were a complex group. They advised educators to develop intentional training programs to enhance learning and reduce stereotypes. The training programs should have been part of faculty development to create awareness about how to minimize assumptions.

Kautsky (1965) discussed Merton's (1948) SFP theory as "a false definition of a situation evoking a new behavior which makes the originally false conception come *true*" (p. 195). In addition to Merton (1948), Brown (2006), Buller (2007), Popp (2005), and Wong and Hui (2006) originally conceptualized the SFP as a contributor to social problems such as racial prejudice, discrimination in education, and the workplace, and economic recessions. Tauber (1997) expanded Merton's definition into five steps, which served as a guide to this qualitative descriptive research study framework.

According to Tauber (1997), the SFP included the following process:

1. Teacher forms expectations.
2. Based upon these expectations, the teacher acts in a differential manner.
3. The teacher's treatment tells each student what behaviors and achievement the teacher expects.
4. If the treatment is consistent over time, and if the student does not actively resist, it will tend to shape his or her behavior and achievement.
5. With time, the student's behavior and achievement will conform more closely to that expected of him or her. (p. 18)

The SFP's *a priori* negative Golem effects expectation framework stereotyped African Americans, especially men, as violent, drug dealers, lazy, and thieves (Hrabowski III et al., 1998; Tauber, 1997). The stereotypes and other negative subtexts categorization of the African American male dated back to the days of slavery (Hrabowski III et al., 1998). According to Hrabowski III et al. (1998), numerous African American men eventually internalized these false stereotypes, which eventually evoked a new behavior, leading to the SFP being put into effect and affecting the men's achievements or underachievements.

The achievement gap literature lacked data that described the experience of Black Deaf male college students (Meadow-Orlans, 2001). The lack of data was a gap that provided researchers insufficient information about the SFP's influence on the educational outcomes of Black Deaf males. The gap in the literature created challenges for institutions that aimed to develop programs to narrow the achievement gap between Black Deaf males, Black hearing males, and their White counterparts.

Definition of Terms

The following definitions were associated with the purpose of this study.

African American and *Black American:* United States citizens of African descent (McCaskill, 2005).

A posteriori: Knowledge based on experience or after an experience (Muller-Merbach, 2007).

A priori: Knowledge based on assumption and not on experience (Muller-Merbach, 2007). In this context, it was preconceived as negative or positive expectations prior to an experience.

Black: An individual who identified himself (the male reference is used here for consistency) as black (McCaskill, 2005).

Black Deaf: A term that implied complexities of cultural dualism between Black and Deaf cultures (McCaskill, 2005).

Cultural dualism: The identification of two complex and dominant cultures used in this context by this researcher, and built on Black and Deaf theoretical frameworks (McCaskill, 2005; Padden & Humphries, 1988).

Deaf: An individual who identified himself as having a hearing loss and identified with Deaf culture (McCaskill, 2005; Padden & Humphries, 1988).

Diaspora: A dispersion of a people, language, or culture that was formerly concentrated in one place (Khoo, 2010). In this context, it was people who shared similar language and culture backgrounds.

Galatea effects: Positive expectations that enhanced a student's achievement (Rubie-Davies et al., 2006).

Golem effects: Negative expectations that impeded a student's achievement (Rubie-Davies et al., 2006).

Descriptive: Research that went beyond statistical explanations to theories by exploring additional multiple external factors associated with perceptions (Creswell, 2005).

Self-fulfilling prophecy: A *false* definition of the situation evoking a new behavior, which makes the original false conception come *true* (Merton, 1948, p. 195).

Assumptions

The first assumption in this qualitative descriptive study was that the study population was representative of the Black Deaf male population at a higher education institution in the Washington, D.C. metropolitan area. The second assumption was that the study participants would be truthful, factual, and open in their responses to the open-ended survey questions. The next assumption was that the study participants maintained and earned a grade point average (GPA) of between 2.0 and 4.0 at the time of graduation.

The GPA was important because Oseguera (2005) found that minority students who persisted to graduation in postsecondary education with all undergraduate coursework earning a C grade or better had a GPA between 2.0 and 4.0. The Black Deaf male student was a minority therefore; this inquiry could identify how he persisted to graduation (U.S. Department of Education, 2010). The final assumption was the results influenced young Black Deaf males, faculty and teachers, leadership of higher education, policy makers, and advocates to be supportive in helping them complete the academic requirements in postsecondary setting.

Scope, Limitations, and Delimitations

Scope. This qualitative descriptive study aimed to examine the SFP influence on Black Deaf male students at a Washington, D.C. University. The study utilized open-ended survey questions to identify teacher expectations, differential treatment, behavior, achievement verbalization, achievement consistency, and time (Tauber, 1997), using themes from Merton's (1948) SFP definition. Theme analysis should have created awareness among Black Deaf male students, faculty and staff and education leadership about the widening achievement gap of this population. This study reviewed existing and historical perspectives of the SFP and administered qualitative survey questions via campus mailboxes, recruitments booths, and the United States Postal Service to Black Deaf male undergraduate students and alumni from a postsecondary institution.

Limitations. The first limitation of this qualitative descriptive study was that this population might have provided biased answers because of preconceived notions about discrimination. The second limitation was that this population might not have articulated the SFP theory. The third, and related, limitation was that the inability to articulate the SFP theory might have influenced the study outcomes. The final limitation pertained to the researcher, who was a Black Deaf male may be biased.

Delimitations. This qualitative descriptive study sought to understand the SFP influence on the postsecondary academic experiences of Black Deaf male students. To this end, the participants were limited to a purposive sample of undergraduate Black Deaf male students and alumni at a university in Washington, D.C. An open-ended survey was administered to the Black Deaf males to explore experiences (Creswell, 2005). This qualitative study aimed to gain a profound understanding of those experiences. The participants must have completed at least one semester of postsecondary education

Summary

The purpose of this qualitative descriptive study was to explore the perceptions of a purposive sample of Black Deaf male students in postsecondary setting in Washington, D.C. to determine if the SFP theory contributed to their pedagogic achievements. Black Deaf male students were selected because they had the lowest graduation rates of any group (Gallaudet University Enrollment Reports, 2008; U.S. Department of Education, 2010). The lack of specific data to explain this academic experience presented a serious problem about factors influencing this population's academic achievements.

According to a 2007 U.S. Department of Education report, 13.2% of Black males with disabilities enrolled in postsecondary education during a 6-year time frame. The report and previous reports similar to it failed to identify Black Deaf male achievement levels. Higher education leadership, policymakers, and advocates should have segregate educational reports and statistics to determine factors that affected the Black Deaf male achievement levels and developed enhancement programs to narrow the gap. Relevant literature and its contribution to social problems such as racial prejudice, and discrimination in education (Brown, 2006) are reviewed in Chapter 2. Racial prejudice and discrimination were foundations of SFP Golem effects (Rubie-Davies et al., 2006). The foundations were false assumptions and expectations that initiate the SFP phenomenon (Rubie-Davies et al., 2006; Tauber, 1997). Cultural dualism and the history of the Black Deaf male were discussed.

Chapter 2

Review of the Literature

The intent of this study was to explore the perceptions of Black Deaf male students in postsecondary setting to determine if the SFP theory contributed to their pedagogic achievements. Black Deaf male students had the lowest graduation rates of any group among approximately 13.2% of Black males with disabilities who enrolled in postsecondary education during a 6-year time frame (Gallaudet University Enrollment Reports 2000-2006; JBHE, 2007; U.S. Department of Education, 2007). The Black Deaf male's achievement was camouflaged within the Black males with disabilities label, which impeded the ability to develop enhancement programs to narrow the achievement gap for these students (U.S. Department of Education, 2010).

Relevant self-fulfilling prophecy literature and its contribution to understanding social problems such as racial prejudice and discrimination in education were reviewed in this chapter (Brown, 2006; Harris, 2005; Jussim & Harber, 2005; Merton, 1948; Rosenthal & Jacobson, 1968; Tauber, 1997). Racial prejudice and discrimination were foundations of Golem effects false assumptions and expectations, which initiated the SFP phenomenon (Harris, 2005; Rubie-Davies et al., 2006; Tauber, 1997). Cultural dualism and the history of the Black Deaf male were contextualized (Guyll, et al., 2010; Johnson & McIntosh, 2009; McCaskill, 2005; Padden & Humphries, 1988).

Documentation and Literature on the SFP Theory

Approximately 500 non-peer-reviewed articles about the SFP theory were examined. The literature review included 136 relevant peer-reviewed articles and 105 dissertations, along with several foundational books and studies relevant to the research topic. Early and current works of Merton, Rosenthal and Jacobson, and Thomas were the foundation for this literature review.

Because of the vast amount of the SFP literature, the selected literature was the most relevant based on historical foundation, author, and relevancy. Despite the large amount of research, there were gaps in the literature that focused on how the SFP influenced the Black Deaf male student's pedagogic experiences. Furthermore, there were gaps in the last 5 years of articles that discussed the SFP relationship to the Black Deaf male student's academic experience.

Literature Review

Historical overview. This qualitative descriptive research study intently explored the *a posteriori* perception of the Black Deaf male student in the postsecondary setting. Available literature on Deaf and Hard of Hearing postsecondary experience categorized this study population under generic, inclusive, camouflaged, and stereotypical labels. The nonspecific categorization and labels created confusion about the Black Deaf male student's educational needs.

In some cases Black Deaf male students were misdiagnosed as mentally retarded and placed in a special education program (Green, 2005; Harris, 2005). The national reports grouped this population under children with hearing loss, Deaf and Hard of Hearing, children with hearing impairment, and Black males with disabilities (Harris 2005; Richardson et al., 2010; U.S. Department of Education, 2007, 2010). Therefore, insufficient research was available that focused on the postsecondary achievements of American Black Deaf male students.

This research theoretical framework represented the SFP historical theories and academic experience and achievement of minorities (Merton, 1948; Tauber, 1997). This investigation was proliferation to the theories with a discussion about the SFP relationship to the academic achievements of Black Deaf male students. The Black Deaf male was historically discussed within minority, Black male with a disability, Deaf and Hard of Hearing, special education, students with learning disabilities, students with disabilities, and mentally retarded theoretical frameworks (James, Kellman, & Lieberman, 2011; Roessler & Foshee, 2010; Salend & Garrick Duhaney, 2005; Troiano, Liefeld, & Trachtenberg, 2010; U.S. Department of Education, 2007, 2010). The generic categorization framework was standard practice at the U.S. Department of Education and established the SFP *a priori* expectations and Golem effects.

The *a priori* expectations and Golem effects framework stereotyped the Black Deaf male academic needs with Black hearing males (Harper & Nichols, 2008). However, Harper and Nichols warned that undergraduate Black males were a complex group that required careful analysis beyond underlying false stereotypes. False stereotypes disguised Black males within minority sub-groups. Sub-groups could have possessed hidden disabilities such as deafness that were inconspicuous to educators (Anderson & Smart, 2010; Merton, 1948; Richardson et al., 2010; Roessler & Foshee, 2010; Tauber, 1997; U.S. Department of Education, 2007, 2010).

Deafness, a hidden disability, could have misguided educators in making incorrect assumptions about a Black male student's educational needs (Mackenzie & Smith, 2009). The erroneous assumption ignored the complex identity needs of the Black male student. The lame postulation was foundation to the Black Deaf male student's cultural dualism and identity theoretical frameworks. The misconceptions of cultural dualism and identity assumption triggered the SFP phenomenon, which influenced the Black Deaf male's educational and social opportunities discussed within the symbolic interactionist, functionalist, and conflict educational theories (Hout, 2011; Pfeiffer & Pfeiffer, 2011; Smit & Fritz, 2008).

The self-fulfilling prophecy. Merton (1948) defined the self-fulfilling prophecy as "a *false* definition of a situation evoking a new behavior which makes the originally false conception come *true*" (p. 195). This research focused on the SFP's influence by exploring the Black Deaf male student's perception on teacher's expectation of his academic abilities, and in return, its influence on his academic achievements. Brown (2006), Buller (2007), Popp (2005), and Wong and Hui (2006) stated that Merton originally conceptualized the SFP as a contributor to social problems. The social problems included racial prejudice, discrimination in education and the workplace, and economic recessions. Tauber (1997) expanded Merton's definition into five steps.

The five steps became the framework for this qualitative descriptive research study with focus on the Black Deaf male's achievement, or lack thereof, in the postsecondary setting. According to Tauber (1997), the SFP occurred when a teacher formed expectations *a priori*. Based upon these expectations, the teacher acted and treated the student in a Golem-effect or Galatea-effect differential manner *a posteriori* (Rubie-Davies et al., 2006; Tsiplakides & Keramida, 2010). The student eventually internalized the differential treating that led to the SFP (Merton, 1948; Rubie-Davies et al., 2006; Tauber, 1997)

The SFP's *a priori* expectations framework stereotyped Blacks, especially men, as violent, drug dealers, lazy, and thieves, and every possible negative subtext dating back to the days of slavery (Hrabowski III et al., 1998; Tauber, 1997). Many Black men eventually internalized these false stereotypes. The stereotypes eventually evoked a new behavior in Black men, and triggered an SFP that influenced their achievements or lack thereof.

The achievement gap literature was void of data that described the college experience for Black Deaf male students (Meadow-Orlans, 2001); therefore, there was no way of knowing that the SFP influenced their educational outcomes. The lack of comprehension about Black Deaf students' low achievement made it challenging to develop programs to narrow the achievement gap between this population, Black hearing males, and their White counterparts. The underpinnings of the SFP phenomenon emerged from the symbolic interactionist educational theory (Crossley, 2010; Merton, 1948; Rosenthal & Jacobson, 1968; Smit & Fritz, 2008; Tauber, 1997).

The symbolic interactionist theorists observed teachers and students during didactic interactions in an academic setting. The scholastic venue was the physical or non-physical fertile atmosphere for knowledge creation through meanings (Crossley, 2010; Smit & Fritz, 2008). The symbolic interactionist and the SFP researchers suggested that negative teacher expectations *a priori* and negative differential treatments *a posteriori* were the foundation of poor academic achievement among minorities (Hinnant et al., 2009; Jussim & Harber, 2005; Merton, 1948; Rosenthal & Jacobson, 1968; Smit & Fritz, 2008; Tauber, 1997).

Comparing and contrasting the symbolic interactionist, functionalist, and conflict educational theories could have shed some light on the research problem (Crossley, 2010;

Smit & Fritz, 2008). The dilemma, however, was the Black Deaf male student's experienced Deaf and Black cultural dualism challenges and overrepresentation in the achievement data, which was susceptible to the SFP phenomenon (McCaskill, 2005; Padden & Humphries, 1988; Skiba et al., 2008). The cultural dualism perspective was congruent with the symbolic interactionist theory and incongruent with the conflict or functionalist theories.

The functionalist speculated that education provided an individual equitable access and opportunities to knowledge for navigating social classes and status (Hout, 2011). The presumption failed to consider factors such as the socioeconomic and political nature of schooling (Patton, 1998). Patton continued in stating that the functionalist theorist should have contemplated "the role played by schools and the special education system in maintaining the existing social and economic stratification order, thereby exerting ideology, social, and political control of African American learners" (p. 27). The functionalist premise also failed to consider the ramifications of the Deaf and Black cultural dualism influence on the Black Deaf male student (McCaskill, 2005; Padden & Humphries, 1988).

The conflict theorist advocated that education should have been reserved for the elites, in-groups, and those with status (Arum et al., 2011; Beaver, 2009). The conflict theorist posited competitiveness in educational attainment toward status that excluded minorities (Beaver, 2009). Patton (1998) warned, "As such, the structures, processes, assumptions, and beliefs of the dominant classes are deeply embedded in the special education knowledge base and its knowledge producers, thus undermining its theory, research, and practice" (p. 27).

The macro-level analysis of the functionalist theorist and the status quo perpetuation of the conflict theorist led to the segregation of minorities and other out-groups, an SFP (Arum et al., 2011; Merton, 1948; Tauber, 1997; Patton, 1998; Rosenthal & Jacobson, 1968). The two theories set expectations that education was reserved for in-group elites and status groups. These in-group elites standards were reinforced with differential treatments of ambiguous educational policies, structures, and assumptions that the symbolic interactionist theorist observed and interpreted as SFP (Arum et al., 2011; Merton, 1948; Patton, 1998; Rosenthal & Jacobson; Smit & Fritz, 2008; Tauber, 1997).

Hout (2011) highlighted that there was a link between educational attainment and employment that perpetuated status and required new lenses as the United States globalized. Hout's point was the basis of the symbolic interactionist theorist. Table 1 illustrates the taxonomy of the educational theories and their implications.

The first column in Table 1 depicts the three educational theories. The second column indicates how the theories influenced social structures in education. The third column identifies the educational theories' *a priori* expectations. The fourth column shows *a posteriori* implications for minorities and Black Deaf male students.

Table 1

Educational Theories and Implications

Educational Theory	Social Level	A priori or A posteriori	Implications for Minorities
Functionalist	Macro and micro	Both	Advocated inclusive education. Set educational policies, and structures that were not equitable to the theories' intent
Conflict	Macro	A posteriori	Excluded minorities and focused on the status quo
Symbolic Interactionist	Micro	Both	Focused on teacher and student didactic interactions, meaning making in the classroom with a special focus on minority achievement

According to Smit and Fritz (2008), the symbolic interactionist theorists observed the sense-making ability of humans within life's social structures and systems. Smit and Fritz (2008) pointed out that the symbolic interactionists observed research participants in a given situation to gain additional insights into social processes and structures within the educational system. Observing research participants had been missing from the functional and conflict theories.

Insights gained from the symbolic interactionist theorist observation were the foundation of the Thomas Theorem (Thomas, 1928). Goar (2009) summarized that the Thomas Theorem was also called the "Definition of the Situation" (p. 1), which described how humans subjectively made sense of and accurately or inaccurately interpreted situations based on social expectations. Goar further stated that Thomas first tested his theorem on poorly unadjusted girls during the pre-industrial period and the industrial revolution.

The unadjusted girls were expected to behave as individuals during the pre-industrial period (Goar, 2009). However, the industrial revolution created new behavioral expectations that led to changes for the unadjusted girls, meaning they conformed their behaviors to the period's expectations. The Thomas test confirmed that societal expectations of the industrial revolution set new expectations for the unadjusted girls that influenced and changed their behavior. Family members of the unadjusted girls interpreted this change to mean that the girls had adopted the industrial revolution societal expectations to become well-adjusted girls, confirming the Thomas Theorem (Thomas, 1928).

Thomas's conclusion, "If men define their situations as real, they are real in the consequences," (p. 9) led to Merton's SFP (Tauber, 1997). Tauber also stated that Merton defined the SFP as "a *false* definition of the situation evoking a new behavior, which makes the original false conception come *true*" (p. 9). Since Merton's conception of the SFP phenomenon, researchers across various disciplines have experimented with and discussed this phenomenon (Amouroux, 2010; De'Armond, 2011; Hershovitz, 2010; Love, 2010; Pinkerton, 2010; Scott, 2010).

The phenomenon was discussed and researched in education because of the widening academic achievement gap and disparities between minorities and Whites (Rosenthal & Jacobson, 1968; Rubie-Davies et al., 2006). The discussion framework was that the SFP was responsible for the widening academic achievement gap because of teacher expectations (Jussim & Harber, 2005; Rosenthal & Jacobson, 1968). Jussim and Harber (2005) and Rosenthal and Jacobson (1968) presented strong evidence that the SFP existed in education.

The issue was not about proof, but rather about stigma consciousness, stereotype threats, and other conditions that fostered negative or positive SFP (Guyll et al., 2010). These conditions were congruent with Merton's (1948) false definition and Tauber's (1997) differential treatments (Guyll et al., 2010). Rubie-Davies et al. (2006) identified a false definition, or Golem effect, and differential treatment condition, or Galatea effects. The Golem was usually negative, and the Galatea was usually positive (Rubie-Davies et al., 2006).

Table 2 correlates the SFP with the Golem and Galatea effects differential treatments. The first column lists Tauber's (1997) five SFP steps. The five SFP steps were the foundation for the Golem and Galatea effects listed in the second and third columns (Rubie-Davies et al., 2006). The Golem and Galatea effects were reinforced by positive or negative teacher differential treatments in the fourth and fifth columns (Rubie-Davies et al., 2006; Tauber, 1997). The Golem and Galatea effects analysis was critical to the student's perception of the classroom experience (Rubie-Davies et al., 2006).

According to Compton-Lily (2011), students perceived teachers as authority figures who should have set good examples, provided a fair, equitable, challenging, and positive learning environment for all. When teachers failed to provide a positive learning environment conducive to respect and high expectations, students tended to adapt their behaviors to fit the setting that led to the SFP (Pfeiffer & Pfeiffer, 2011). The key to the SFP theory was not the negative implications, but that awareness of the SFP should have guided broader, dynamic, and positive educational reforms (Hawes 2005).

Table 2

Golem and Galatea Effects, and Differential Treatments (DT)

Five SFP Steps	Golem Effect	Galatea Effect	DT Negative	DT Positive
Teacher forms expectations	Subconsciously lowered expectation	Subconsciously raised expectation	Negative expectation	Positive expectation
Based upon these expectations, the teacher acts in a differential manner	Conveyed the expectation consciously or subconsciously	Conveyed the expectation consciously or subconsciously	Ignorant and callous body language	Attentive and warmhearted body language
The teacher's treatment tells each student what behaviors and achievement the teacher expects	Modeled a negative behavior and used verbal persuasion	Modeled a positive behavior and used verbal persuasion	Negative reinforcement that confirms negative expectation	Positive reinforcement that confirms the positive expectation
If the treatment is consistent over time, and if the student does not actively resist, it will shape his or her behavior and achievement	Dismissed the opportunity to use proven techniques to reinforce the subconscious expectation leading to failure	Used proven techniques to reinforce the subconscious expectation to ensure success	Low grades and disciplinary actions that are consistent with the negative expectation	Good grades and positive recommendations to colleagues that are consistent with the positive expectation
With time, the student's behavior and achievement will conform more closely to that expected of him or her	Expected negative behavior conforms with subconscious expectation	Expected behavior conforms with subconscious expectation	Negative SFP	Positive SFP

Note: DT = Differential Treatments; SFP = self-fulfilling prophecy

Current Findings

Several researchers offered divergent views of the SFP effects on the academic performance of students (Al-Fadhi & Singh, 2006; Couch, 2010; Jussim & Harber, 2005; Riley & Ungerleider, 2008; Rubie-Davies et al., 2006; Rubie-Davies, Peterson, Irving, Widdowson, & Dixon, 2010; Tsiplakides & Keramida, 2010; Willard, Madon, Guyll, Spoth, & Jussim, 2008; Wong & Hui, 2006). These researchers were concerned that SFP research had focused on Golem effects (Rubie-Davies et al., 2006). The researchers expressed concerns that the views depicting negative teachers' expectations influence on a student's achievement were potentially not true.

For example, Rubie-Davies et al. (2006) found evidence of other possible variables that went beyond the Golem effects perspective to consider in the SFP research discussion. The educational experience was a dyadic relationship between the teacher and student in a dynamic and complex environment fraught with inequalities, disparities, and regulations (Balfanz, Legtere, West, & Weber, 2007; Breen, 2010; Sears, 2008; Skiba et al., 2008). One such instance was how government regulations and expectations involving legislation like the No Child Left Behind Act (NCLB) of 2001 could have influenced educational outcomes (Balfanz et al., 2007). The NCLB was congruent with the functional and conflict educational theories (Patton, 1998; Smit & Fritz, 2008).

The four NCLB provisions were stronger accountability for results, record flexibility for states and communities, concentrating resources on proven education methods, and more choices for parents (Balfanz et al., 2007; Hunter & Bartee, 2003). These governmental expectations added complexity to the achievement gap discussion, pressured teachers, and challenged educational leadership (Balfanz et al., 2007). These expectations, however, were not discussed in the Golem effect point of view in the SFP literature (Hinnant et al., 2009; Rubie-Davies et al., 2006).

Nieto (2009) offered another perspective: the SFP research should have considered school culture and climate factors. Culture and climate were dynamic and complex variables because each was associated with expectations (Nieto, 2009). Nieto pointed out that a school climate was a learning environment with clear expectations of what behaviors were accepted, or unaccepted, and rewarded, or unrewarded. Personal growth and rules of conduct were part of the school climate expectations; the personal growth and conduct of students were contingent on teacher review and expectations (Nieto, 2009).

Therefore, a teacher who lacked knowledge and understanding about the Black Deaf male student's cultural and ethnicity challenges within the school climate could have imposed personal growth and climate expectations Golem effects on him (Guyll et al., 2010; McCaskill, 2005; Nieto, 2009; Padden & Humphries, 1988). A school's culture includes the norms, beliefs, values, rituals, ceremonies and traditions shaped through its history and participants (Nieto, 2009). Teachers and students become part of the school culture over time and behaved as expected. These expectations were congruent with the Thomas (1928) experiment and the Golem-effect point of view that could have influenced teachers and students educational experiences (Rubie-Davies et al., 2006).

In contrast, some researchers argued that the SFP research failed to support expected hypotheses (Becker, 2010; Hinnant et al., 2009; Jussim & Harber, 2005). They speculated that earlier SFP research induced perceptual biases in the laboratory, which affected the outcomes. Hinnant et al. (2009) indicated also that SFP research hypothesized mixed findings, which caused inconsistency in the literature regarding support for Golem-effect and Galatea-effect perspectives (Rubie-Davies et al., 2006).

The Golem-effect perspective found in the literature contended that expectations of teachers *a priori* usually had negative implications influencing the achievement gap of certain groups or all (Becker 2010; Rosenthal & Jacobson, 1968). According to Rubie-Davies et al. (2006), the Golem-effect characterization "includes gender, ethnicity, social class, stereotypes, diagnostic labels, physical attractiveness, language style, the age of the student, personality and social skills, the relationship between teacher and student background, names, other siblings and one-parent background" (p. 430). Finally, the Golem-effect perspective contended that negative teacher expectations were reinforced by negative differential treatment (Rubie-Davies et al., 2006; Tauber, 1997).

In contrast to the Golem effects were the Galatea effects (Rubie-Davies et al., 2006). The Galatea-effect literature argued that positive teacher expectations, and other variables such as verbal praise and other external rewards, should have been considered (Rubie-Davies et al., 2006). Galatea-effect supporters speculated that formative feedback was *a posteriori*, improved the student's learning experience (Rubie-Davies et al., 2006).

The two divergent views on the Golem effects and the Galatea effects of the SFP and teacher expectations on student achievement focused on Black hearing minorities, White hearing students, and students from low-socioeconomic backgrounds (de Boer, Bosker & van der Werf, 2010; Green, 2005; Guyll et al., 2010; Rubie-Davies et al., 2006). None focused on Black Deaf male students. Hinnant et al. (2009) found that "Minority boys had the lowest performance when their abilities were underestimated

[Golem effect] and the greatest gains when their abilities were overestimated [Galatea effect]" (p. 669).

Skiba et al. (2008) stated, "The disproportionate representation of minority students is among the most critical and enduring problems in the field of education" (p. 264). This sentiment was central to the SFP and achievement gap arguments that government policies failed consistently to result in substantial changes. The lack of changes perpetuated the functionalist and conflict theories on the macro level and benefited elite in-group members with status (Hout, 2011).

Scarce literature discussions were available about the SFP influences and teacher expectations of Black Deaf male students (Williamson, 2007). Available literature generalized or misdiagnosed Black Deaf male students under various generic disability labels: exceptional children, hearing impaired students, students with disabilities, and mentally retarded (Ferri & Conor, 2005; Green, 2005; Skiba et al., 2008). These labels limited opportunities to research the complex cultural dualism influence on their educational experience and achievement (Guyll et al., 2010; McCaskill, 2005; Padden & Humphries, 1988).

The cultural dualism perspective could have revealed coping strategies in the postsecondary setting for this population. Leadership in education could have assimilated the cultural dualism perspective into curriculum development. Absorbing the perspective could have narrowed or equalized the achievement gap for Black Deaf males and other minority students.

The self-fulfilling prophecy and academic achievement. According to Tauber (1997), the SFP theory caught the attention of educators with the publication of *Teacher*

Expectations for the Disadvantaged by Rosenthal and Jacobson (1968). Rosenthal and Jacobson used an experiment to manipulate expectations teachers had of their students. They administered a school-wide test to randomly selected bloomers (experimental group) and non-bloomers (control group). A re-admission test at the end of the school year showed that bloomers experienced intellectual gains (achievement). The researchers told the teachers that bloomers were good students; this established the teacher's *a priori* expectation.

In interviews, the teachers described the bloomers as happier, successful, curious, interested, better adjusted, and more affectionate than the non-bloomers. The researchers concluded that the SFP was evident because expectancy confirmation, regardless of whether the initial expectation was erroneous or true, evoked performance outcomes consistent with the initial expectations (Wilson & Stephens, 2007). Eiser, Stafford, and Fazio (2008) added that the expectancy confirmation was not about the student's performance, but about the teacher's mental state. The concept of mental state was comparable to mental models (Senge, 1990) and was critical to the SFP.

Senge (1990) defined mental models as "deeply ingrained assumptions, generalizations, or even pictures or images that influence how we understand the world and how we take action. Very often we are not consciously aware of our mental models or effects they have on behavior" (p. 8). The mental models concept was a powerful analogical tool that offered comparative analysis of the SFP and the five class, race, and achievement realities (Ornstein & Levine, 1989) (Table 3). The five realities were differences in teacher and student backgrounds, teacher perceptions of student inadequacy, low standard of performance, ineffective instructional grouping, and difficult teaching conditions.

Table 3

The Five Race, Class, and Achievement Realities, and Implications

The Five SFP Steps	The Five Class, Race, and Achievement Realities	Implications
Teacher forms expectations	Differences in teacher/student background	Lack of teacher understanding of student background led to pre-conceived low expectations
Based upon these expectations, the teacher acts in a differential manner	Teacher perceptions of student inadequacy	Pre-conceived low expectations led to differential treatments
The teacher's treatment tells each student what behaviors and achievement the teacher expects	Low standard of performance expectations	Pre-conceived low expectations and differential treatments were acceptable to teachers
If the treatment is consistent over time, and if the student does not actively resist, it will tend to shape his or her behavior and achievement	Ineffective instructional grouping	Teachers segregated students based on the pre-conceived low expectations
With time, the student's behavior and achievement will conform more closely to that expected of him or her	Difficult teaching conditions	Pre-conceived low expectations led to extreme behavior problems among the student: SFP

Note: SFP=self-fulfilling prophecy

The first column of Table 3 lists the five SFP steps (Tauber, 1997). The second column lists the five class, race, and achievement realities (Ornstein & Levin, 1989). The first and second columns compare and build on the teacher's mental model (Senge, 1990). A teacher's negative or positive mental model could influence a student's academic experience because a teacher is an authority figure that students look to for guidance (Wooley & Bowen, 2007).

Students looked up to teachers as authority figures in classrooms as to how they were treated and positive learning environments. When teachers failed to provide positive learning environments that reflected respect and high expectations, students tended to adapt their behaviors to fit the setting, and this adaption stunted their achievement and learning (Rubie-Davies et al., 2006; Wooley & Bowen, 2007). Senge (1990) advised that leaders and authority figures such as teachers should have exercised and disciplined his or her mental models. The ability to subject personal mental models to rigorous scrutiny with balanced inquiry and advocacy could have created a positive organizational and academic learning environment (Senge, 1990). The symbolic interactionist aimed to observe the intricacies of the teacher's mental model and its influence on the student's learning (Senge, 1990; Smit & Fritz, 2008).

The self-fulfilling prophecy and learning. *According to Rosenthal and Jacobson (1968), when teachers established high expectations, student learning, and achievement increased. Tauber (1997) outlined the SFP's five steps and their implications for learning. The five steps are: (1) teacher forms expectations, (2) based on these expectations, the teacher acts in a differential manner, (3) the teacher's treatment tells each student what behavior and achievement the teacher expects, (4) if this treatment is consistent over time, and if the student does not actively resist, it will tend to shape his or her behavior and achievement, and (5) with time, the student's behavior and achievement will conform more closely to that expected of him or her.*

Step 1: Teacher forms expectations. A number of researchers indicated that a teacher's expectations affected student learning (de Boer et al., 2010; Merton, 1948; Rosenthal & Jacobson, 1968; Tauber, 1997). The expectancy effect operated during dyadic interactions between the teacher and the student. However, the critical component of teacher expectations affecting student learning was the teacher's actions (McIntyre, 2007).

Eiser et al. (2008) added that the expectancy confirmation was not about the student's performance, but rather the teacher's mental state or mental models (Senge, 1990). McIntyre, Kyle, and Moore (2006), as did Eiser et al. (2008), implied that a teacher's mental state could have influenced his or her actions toward the student in the dyadic interaction. The teacher's actions began the SFP and could have influenced the students' learning in a positive way if the teacher had positive expectations, or a negative way if the teacher had negative expectations (Tauber, 1997).

Step 2: Based upon these expectations, the teacher acts in a differential manner. Tauber (1997) outlined the four-factor theory about differential treatments that conveyed expectations in a learning environment. Table 4 characterizes the four-factor theory (climate, feedback, input, output) and implications for learning. The classroom environment was fertile for knowledge creation and dyadic interactions between the teacher and student (Brown, Mangelsdorf, Neff, Schoppe-Sullivan, & Frosch, 2009). The SFP could have influenced teacher and student positively or negatively during didactic interaction in the classroom.

The teacher-student interaction was an opportunity for the teacher and the student to capitalize on feedback (Tauber, 1997). Feedback quality and quantity were important.

The feedback quality meant that the teacher provided detailed remarks that helped a student's critical thinking development. Equally important was the feedback quantity, meaning the teacher was consistent and persistent with all students.

Table 4

The Four-factor Theory and Implications for Learning

The Four-factor Theory	Implications for Learning
Climate	The environment conducive to learning – could have been positive or negative, supportive or unsupportive, high expectations or low expectations
Feedback	Affective and cognitive reinforcements – quality and quantity reinforcement was given to all students equally
Input	Teacher's attention spread – the teacher provided equal teaching attention to all students regardless of ability or disability
Output	Verbal and nonverbal cues – The teacher prompted, probed, and gave the opportunity to all students to learn

The first column in Table 4 is Tauber's (1997) four-factor theory and the second column provides the implications for learning. Climate was a prolific environment for knowledge creation. The climate concept in the four-factor theory was congruent with the functionalist theory that education should have been for all in a high expectation environment (Patton, 1998).

Feedback complemented the Galatea-effect point of view, which supported the functionalist equitable educational theoretical framework (Patton, 1998; Rubie-Davies et al., 2006). The input was the quality and quantity of the teaching, an indication that the teacher taught the subject equally to all students by offering one-on-one attention equitably. Equitable teaching, quality and quantity feedback contrasted with the conflict theory and compared to the functionalist theory (Patton, 1998). There should have not been indication that perceived high-performing students or elite students received better teaching than perceived low-performing students in the functionalist macro analysis (Beaver, 2009; Hout, 2011).

Output was the verbal and nonverbal outcomes observed and interpreted using the symbolic interactions theory to determine student learning outcomes, or the student's perception of the teacher (Rubie-Davies, 2006; Smit & Fritz, 2008). According to Rubie-Davies (2010), students observed the teacher's differential treatment through verbal and nonverbal outputs. An example of verbal output was when the teacher probed perceived high performers with cues that triggered different answers but did not probe perceived low performers. An example of nonverbal output was when the teacher's used body language such as smiling toward perceived high performers but not smiling with perceived low performers in the didactic interaction (Brown et al., 2009).

Step 3: The teacher's treatment tells each student what behaviors and achievement the teacher expects. The four-factor theory (Table 4) establishes the tone for acceptable and unacceptable classroom behaviors (Tauber, 1997). Eventually, students began to internalize the teacher's expectations because the four-factor theory was stimulus in the didactic interaction (Brown et al., 2009). The stimulus sent clear messages to students about which behaviors were acceptable to achievement and learning. A student could have deciphered expectations set by authority figures regardless of verbal or nonverbal cues to modify his or her behavior (Tauber, 1997).

The functionalist and conflict theories focused on the macro level interaction between educational organizations and society with little attention to how the teacher and student behaved in the classroom (Hout, 2011). The symbolic interactionist theory proposed that researchers should have observed the teacher-student interaction and behaviors in the classroom to examine learning or lack of learning (Smit & Fritz, 2008). The students behavior adjustment was a component of the SFP defined by Merton (1948) as "a *false* definition of the situation evoking a new behavior, which makes the original false conception come *true*" (Tauber, 1997, p. 9) depending on the consistency of the differential treatment.

Step 4: If this treatment is consistent over time, and if the student does not actively resist, it will tend to shape his or her behavior and achievement. The classroom was an environment conducive to dyadic interaction that provided stability for learning (Brown et al., 2009). The classroom environment was also an opportunity for teachers to be consistent with Galatea effects of differential treatment and feedback (Rubie-Davies et al., 2006). Feedback was critical to a student's learning and development (Tauber, 1997).

Students began receiving feedback and praise from parents at birth and began internalizing that parents were authority figures similar to teachers (Rubie-Davies, 2010). Parents instilled in children the expectation to show respect to authority figures. Children learned to respect and value a teacher's feedback. Rubie-Davies (2010) advised that feedback was critical to learning.

The functionalists viewed feedback in the form of a reward for adhering to educational schedules, following school rules, and respecting authority (Patton, 1998). The conflict theorist was not concerned with feedback to promote learning; the focus was on creating access to top quality learning environment for in-groups and the elites (Beaver, 2009). The symbolic interactionist was concerned with positive feedback in the learning environment (Smit & Fritz, 2008).

For most children, learning took place in both home and school environments. These learning environments should have been free of Golem effects expectations so that Galatea effects feedback positively influenced the child's development and learning (Tauber, 1997). Rubie-Davies (2006) concluded that teachers and parents should have encouraged [give feedback] their children to set high expectations for themselves.

A consistent positive expectation and feedback could have shaped a student's behavior, learning, and achievement (Rubie-Davies, 2010; Tauber, 1997; Usher, 2009). Tauber (1997) warned that children were at risk of believing a teacher's consistent evaluations because the teacher played a major role in influencing how a child thought about him or herself and his or her abilities. The teacher's role was critical in shaping the child's learning, especially minority children (Blacks) because he or she was a role model to the child (Anderson & Miller, 2004; Hrabowski III et al., 1998).

Step 5: With time, the student's behavior and achievement will conform more closely to that expected of him or her. When children believed in the teacher's consistent evaluations, he or she began to internalize and behave in ways that confirmed the teacher's expectations (Tauber, 1997). The key was the teacher's treatment before, during, and after the evaluation process (Rubie-Davies, 2006). Rubie-Davies (2006) found evidence "that student self-perception in academic areas did alter across the year in accordance with teachers' expectations for their classes is an important one and has implications for practicing teachers as well as for perspective teacher education programs" (p. 550). The finding was an indication that students conformed to the SFP with varied achievements that were complementary to the teacher's expectation and treatment.

The conflict theorist was not concerned with Rubie-Davies' (2006) findings because the theory focused on the elites (Beaver, 2009). The functionalist theorist rhetorically advocated that an education was a necessity for skill development toward a successful occupation (Beaver, 2009). The symbolic interactionist theorist observed how educational activities between the teacher and students took place in the classroom to understand the educational outcomes (Smit & Fritz, 2008). The outcomes of several SFP research studies proposed that the phenomenon influenced life choices (Rosenthal & Jacobson, 1968).

The self-fulfilling prophecy and life choices. Caufield (2007) found that the SFP and life choices were closely related to the concept of expectancy. According to Caufield (2007), the choices we make are dependent on our belief system [*a prior* false or true definition] and those choices are guided by past outcomes [*a posteriori* feedback], which boost our confidence to continue making those choices. He also added that a teacher's positive or negative feedback motivates students to behave in a certain ways. This definition is congruent with Merton's SFP definition that "In the beginning, a *false* definition of the situation evoking a new behavior, which makes the original false conception come *true*" (Tauber, 1997, p. 9).

Numerous researchers discussed the two concepts and their influence on academic achievement and education as a vehicle to life choices (Hout, 2011; Rosenthal & Jacobson, 1968). Life choice was broadly defined as the ability to filter complex information to make informed decisions about life, and the use of a role model to influence those decisions (Anderson & Miller, 2004). Informed decisions ranged from buying a car to finding a career and have been associated with education and achievement. The idea that a more educated person has access to information that guides life choice was the foundation of the functionalist and conflict theories (Hout, 2011).

The university influence on occupational mobility was dependent on the ability to graduate students (Brown, 2006). The ability or inability to graduate had been the central argument of the SFP because minority students were not expected to graduate (Hrabowski III et al., 1998; Tauber, 1997). Poor graduation rates or achievement stemmed from Golem effect expectations and were evident in the literature (Darling-Hammond, 2004; Merton, 1948; Rosenthal & Jacobson, 1968; Tauber, 1997).

For example, Darling-Hammond (2004) discussed serious disparities in educational opportunities in *The Color Line in American Education: Race, Resources, and Student Achievement*. The author pointed out that after 50 years, *Brown v. Board of Education* appeared hopeless because the case had not made a significant dent in equalizing educational opportunities for minorities; instead, the case continued to reinforce the functionalist and conflict theories.

Darling-Hammond (2004) specifically pointed out:

> For Americans of all backgrounds, the allocation of opportunity in a society that is becoming ever more dependent on knowledge and education is a source of great anxiety and concern, exacerbating debates about who is entitled to high quality educational opportunities at every level of schooling. (p. 214)

The lack of access to high quality and equitable educational opportunities limited minorities' potential life choices, perpetuated the SFP, and promoted the functionalist and conflict theories (Hout, 2010; Hrabowski III et al., 1998). Life choices were dependent on the influence of a positive role model to guide minority students' academic achievement (Anderson & Miller, 2004). Mandara, Varner, Greene, and Richman (2009) advised that the current educational system should have been assessed for the influence of family factors such as role models on students' academic achievement and life choices.

Numerous studies existed about the positive influence of role models on the educational experience of students, the ability to navigate the complex academic environment, and on academic achievement (Bembenutty, 2008; Mandara et al., 2009). Mandara et al. (2009) found that parental involvement was critical to their children's academic transition because parents served as role models. "Most people who make positive life choices and experience success in school or work have at least one person who cares about them" (Anderson & Miller, 2004, pp. 29-30). That person who cared often set expectations of success and behaved in ways (with positive differential treatment and feedback) to fulfill the expectation (see Table 5).

Table 5 is a taxonomy of the five SFP steps and role model relationship, illustrating a positive outcome. The role model followed the five SFP steps by beginning with a discussion about expectations. Through the discussion, behavioral expectations were set with accountability parameters. The accountability parameters described specific expected actions that constituted success or failure (achievement of the expectations). The role model provided verbal and nonverbal reinforcement, support, and constructive criticism throughout this process. Support varied until the student reached the expected achievement outcome.

Table 5

Five SFP Steps and Role Model Behaviors

Five SFP Steps	Role Model Behaviors
Teacher forms expectations	Mutually established expectations
Based upon these expectations, the teacher acts in a differential manner	Established accountability parameters and behavioral expectations
The teacher's treatment tells each student what behaviors and achievement the teacher expects	Verbal and nonverbal reinforcement, support, constructive criticism and reminder of accountability
If the treatment is consistent over time, and if the student does not actively resist, it will tend to shape his or her behavior and achievement	Persistent verbal and nonverbal reinforcement, support, constructive criticism
With time, the student's behavior and achievement will conform more closely to that expected of him or her	Positive accomplishments and academic achievement

Note: SFP = self-fulfilling prophecy

The positive outcome should have been the goal of closing the achievement gap that led to successful graduation and optimal life choices. However, the literature revealed serious disparities that continued to hinder equitable educational opportunities, achievement, and role model availability for minorities (Baxley, 2008; Darling-Hammond, 2004). The disparities and lack of role models often led to poor life choices (Hrabowski III et al., 1998). Hrabowski III et al. (1998) added, "only 33% of all Black children under the age of 18 are living with both parents—a marked decrease over the previous generation when 59% were living with both mother and father" (p. 25).

Cosby and Poussaint (2007) found some startling data about the consequences for black men who lacked role models, reported that:

> Young black men are twice as likely to be unemployed as White,
> Hispanic, and Asian men. Although black people make up just 12% of the
> general population, they make up nearly 44% of the prison population. At
> any given time, as many as one in four of all young black men are in the
> criminal justice system – in prison or jail, on probation, or on parole. By
> the time they reach their mid-30s, 6 out of 10 black high school dropouts
> have spent time in prison. About one-third of the homeless are black men.
> (p. 9)

Cosby and Poussaint's (2007) statistics were heavily influenced by educational disparities and lack of role models to guide minorities, especially Black men's, life choices. One particular group of minority students focused in this research was the Black Deaf male student population. The next section discusses the history of Black Deaf and Hard of Hearing males grounded in the Deaf and Black culture perspective.

History of Deaf and Hard of Hearing Black Males

The history of Black Deaf and Hard of Hearing males is embedded within the history of Black hearing males (McCaskill, 2005; Padden & Humphries, 1988). For example, White hearing males were first to gain citizenship in America, meaning historical information about Black Deaf males is encrusted within White hearing, White Deaf, and Black hearing history (McCaskill, 2005). The prioritization of Whites in American history were central to unemployment rates and educational disparities, stigma consciousness, stereotype threats, segregation in housing, emphasis on minority students in lower tracks curricular, and achievement gap comparisons in the literature (Cosby & Poussaint, 2007; Darling-Hammond, 2004; Guyll et al., 2010; Hrabowski III et al., 1998).

The prioritization of the White hearing community was the same as the prioritization of White Deaf people in the literature and reinforced the conflict theory in the Deaf community (Hout, 2011). The literature focused on White issues and considered Whites as social elites and in-groups, or conflict theorist-oriented (Beaver, 2009). A clear understanding of this conflict theorist should have guided the analysis of the milestones of Black Deaf and Hard of Hearing experiences from a historical and achievement perspective (Buchanan, 1999; McCaskill, 2005).

According to Buchanan (1999), "The history of most Deaf Americans prior to 1800 is undocumented" (p. 1). Van Cleve and Crouch (1989) and Padden and Humphries (1988) found that Deaf history was first documented in 1779 in France. Padden and Humphries (1988) indicated that the first school for the Deaf in the world was established around 1761. Van Cleve and Crouch (1989) further found that France was the only country where Deaf and hearing interactions were documented in the late eighteenth and early nineteenth centuries. The first formal recognition of the emergence of Deaf people in the United States was at Martha's Vineyard where Deaf and hearing citizens integrated in all aspects of life (Van Cleve & Crouch, 1989).

The Deaf and hearing citizens of Martha's Vineyard communicated in sign language and married each other until the late eighteenth and the nineteenth centuries, which spawned cultural units and communities in response to historical developments. The historical developments led to scattered documentation of Deaf history (Van Cleve & Crouch, 1989). Scattered documentation of Deaf history created a challenge for researchers in collecting and analyzing that group's experiences and educational achievements (Padden & Humphries, 1988; Van Cleve & Crouch, 1989). Therefore, other groups such as Black Deaf people found their histories undocumented. Table 6 provides a chronological history of White Deaf individuals in America that does not account for Black Deaf individuals.

Table 6

Chronological History of Deaf Individuals

Year	Location	Documentation	Race/Ethnicity
1761	France	First school for the Deaf in the world	White
1779	France	Parisian Deaf community	White
1800	America	Martha's Vineyard	White
1817	America	First school for the Deaf in America	White
1800-1850	America	Two schools for the Deaf founded	White
1850-1875	America	Seven schools for the Deaf founded	White
1864	America	National Deaf Mute College founded (Gallaudet University)	White
1875-1900	America	13 schools for the Deaf founded	White
1900	America	40,000 citizens	White

According to Buchanan (1999), in the 1900s, Deaf leaders seeking educational reform focused on White males and excluded women and minorities. Buchanan made key observations about the educational disparities and practices that persist today and influences the achievement gap of Black Deaf and Hard of Hearing males. Buchanan's (1999) observations had subtle undertones of the functionalist and conflict theories, which showed the need for the symbolic interactionist theoretical frameworks (Crossley, 2010; Smit, & Fritz, 2008).

Buchanan (1999) observed:

In addition, racially biased practices often neglected or excluded Deaf African American children just as gender-biased assumptions narrowed Deaf women's educational opportunities. At national conventions held in the latter half of the century, few teachers and administrators, whether

> Deaf or hearing, even mentioned African American students, although a
> handful of White community-based leaders intermittently advocated
> improving their schools. (p. 7)

Buchanan's observations represented a critical analysis of the Black Deaf male plight with regard to the achievement gap until 1952 (Jowers, 2005). Jowers (2005) documented that *Miller v. Board of Education of District of Columbia* spotlighted the educational disparities prior to the *Brown v. Board of Education* case (Sears, 2008). The *Miller v. Board of Education of District of Columbia* case challenged the District practice of sending Black Deaf children to Maryland School for the Colored Deaf (MSCD). MSCD was outside the jurisdiction for providing education to District residents, which violated the 1905 Congressional legislation.

Jowers (2005) added that the *Miller v. Board of Education of District of Columbia* case was the only advocacy case to challenge educational segregation. The case heightened leaders' awareness about the educational disparities and low achievement among Black Deaf individuals. However, the problem has persisted even today, and significantly affected Black Deaf males' achievements.

Current literature discussion about educational disparities and achievement gap began dissecting the functionalist and conflict theories through the symbolic interactionist lens to reveal the ineffectiveness of the Individuals with Disabilities Act (IDEA), No Child Left Behind (NCLB), and the Americans with Disabilities Act (ADA) (Darling-Hammond, 2004; Hunter & Bartee, 2003; Matthews, 2005). For example, IDEA, NCLB and ADA were public policies created to close the achievement gap between Whites and blacks. However, these policies and others similar continued to fail to meet the educational needs of minorities and Black Deaf males because historically the laws focused on the White hearing male's educational needs and supported the conflict theory (Beaver, 2009; Darling-Hammond, 2004; Hunter & Bartee, 2003; Matthews, 2005).

Matthews (2005) pointed out that the No Child Left Behind Act (NCLB) was criticized for failing to attain equitable educational outcomes for all students proponent to the functionalist theory (Patton, 1998). The NCLB standard testing might have been a good idea but failed to address the student's preparation inadequacies revealed through the symbolic interactions observation of teacher-student classroom interactions (Darling-Hammond, 2004). Preparation was the key to closing the achievement gap because poor student preparation was like a poor foundation to a house; a house built on poor foundation was bound to collapse eventually.

Hunter and Bartee (2003) outlined the four provisions of the NCLB Act intended to foster stronger accountability for results, record flexibility for states and communities, concentrate resources on proven education methods, and offer more choices for parents. The four NCLB provisions were bound to the SFP like a domino effect because the provisions established expectations of leadership. Leadership, in turn, recognized expectations among teachers. Teachers then formed expectations of students to pass standardized tests to meet provision requirements, reinforcing the conflict theory because the NCLB testing provision was found to serve the elite and in-groups (Darling-Hammond, 2004; Hunter & Bartee, 2003; Matthews, 2005).

The NCLB provisions domino effect created expectations that reinforced the conflict theory when the needs and achievement of Black Deaf males were nonexistent in the educational paradigm (Anderson & Miller, 2004; McCaskill, 2005). Buchanan

(1999) found that only few Deaf male leaders paid attention to women and minorities' rights during educational reforms. Incidentally, a pragmatic analysis of the NCLD, ADA, and IDEA revealed that Buchanan's observations (prophecies) persisted or were fulfilled. Educational policy changed had to begin with clear understanding of the history, and background of Black Deaf male's cultural dualism, and ethnicity identification.

Dualism of culture and identity development—Deaf and Black. The Black Deaf male faced difficult cultural dualism challenges that have not been widely discussed in achievement gap research literature (Guyll et al., 2010). The first challenge was the acknowledgment that nearly everyone in society identified an individual based on his or her skin color prior to forming an opinion. The conflict theory built a case by identifying Whites as elite and in-group but didn't consider the Black Deaf male student or other minorities (Beaver, 2009). The functionalist theory perspective was that education was for everyone when in practice the theory was congruent with the conflict theory (Beaver, 2009).

The Black Deaf male was seen first as Black male and then as Deaf, and encountered biases and discrimination associated with a Black male and Deaf identities. Guyll et al. (2010) added, "Ethnic identity conveys one's attachment to their ethnic group, indicating how positive and important group membership is to the individual" (p. 115). The Black Deaf individual was immersed in Black and Deaf cultures, which could have raised identity questions. A clear understanding of culture and identity questions could have shed light on ways to close the achievement gap, the goal of the symbolic interactionist theory (Smit & Fritz, 2008).

The second challenge was that Deafness was a hidden disability (Mackenzie & Smith, 2009). One cannot identify a Deaf or a hearing person at first glance unless the Deaf person is wearing a hearing aid, had a cochlear implant, or used American Sign Language (ASL) to communicate (McCaskill, 2005). Failure to identify a Black male as Deaf at the onset created a problem for educators and education leadership developing programs to help the student succeed in school (McCaskill, 2005).

The use of a hearing aid is another challenge for Deaf individuals. A misconception is that hearing aids help Deaf individuals hear and speak (National Institute on Deafness and Other Communication Disorders [NID.C.D], 2007). Hearing aids amplifies sound for Deaf individuals with mild hearing loss but are ineffective for those with severe hearing loss (NID.C.D, 2007). NID.C.D (2007) stated there is no evidence that hearing aids improve hearing and speech. These created some barriers to the development of the Black Deaf male identity. The psychological, sociological, social psychological, and human and development ecology literatures laid the groundwork for examining the cultural dualism identity development of Black Deaf males (DeCuir-Gunby, 2009; Erickson, 1968; Josselson, 1987; Renn, 2008; Torres, Jones, & Renn, 2009).

Psychology and identity development. According to Erickson (1968), Sigmund Freud was first to conceptualize individual and group identity development. Freud hypothesized that identity was an individual's ability to identify as self, interact within his or her group and outside of that group (Erickson, 1968). In short, identity was the ability to fit in one's own group and successfully interact outside that group with others.

This process was critical to personality development (Erickson, 1968), who added, "A healthy personality actively masters his environment, shows a certain unity of personality, and is able to perceive the world and himself correctly" (p. 51). The functionalist and conflict theories failed to take identity into consideration or assumed that students had already developed identity (Patton, 1998; Weaver & Agle, 2002). The symbolic interactionist goal was to observe interactions between teacher-students in the classroom to shed some light about the factors the influenced minority achievement (Smit & Fritz, 2008).

Black and Deaf. According to Erickson's (1968) identity development definition, the Black Deaf male has a dual identity: Black and Deaf. This dual identity creates a challenge for the Black Deaf male child because of the complexity of both identities (Guyll et al., 2010). Guyll et al. (2010) cited that researchers "found greater ethnic identity to be associated with better academic performance and attitudes" (p. 115). Conceptually, the Black Deaf male child may be confused about his identity when compared with a Black hearing male (McCaskill, 2005). One reason for the confusion is communication barriers during the formative years, which creates barriers to achievement in school and life (Guyll et al., 2010).

The types of confusion should have been considered in the functionalist and conflict educational theories literature to guide social classes and structures discourse (Beaver, 2009; Weaver & Agle, 2002). Erickson (1968) surmised that individuals developed identity or personality through a series of dyadic and intergroup interactions during formative and adolescence years and young adulthood. An individual's developed identity or personality was critical in his or her late adolescence years (Erickson, 1968).

This was the time when young adults built confidence to become self-sustaining adults through family support, peer acceptance and support, and teacher expectations, and validation regarding academic achievement (Erickson, 1968).

The Black Deaf male cultural dualism identity was contingent to role model support systems that were often insufficient (Anderson & Miller, 2004). Guyll et al. (2010) advised, "It is equally important to educate teachers, administrators, and other school personal [who serve as role models] about ways to avoid creating or otherwise contributing to these harmful effects" (p. 126). Sarant et al. (2008) surmised that parents of Deaf children should have been effective communicators with their children to guide cultural dualism identity development along with the ability to identify a role model.

According to Sarant et al., (2008), research indicated that Deaf children learned language "only at 50%-60% of the rate of children with normal hearing and have at least one year language delay by the time they are school age" (p. 205). Language delay influenced the Black Deaf male's ability to compete for resources, and educational and social opportunities and led to poor academic performance in the classroom (Sarant et al., 2008; McCaskill, 2005). The classroom was a social setting and the fertile ground for learning in which effective communication provided access to resources and personal achievement, which influenced a student's social and identity development (Sarant et al., 2008).

Sociology and identity development. Identity development in the social setting was a dynamic and complex process in the dyadic and intergroup interactions such as identity politics and social movements (Torres et al., 2009). The complexity within this process was one's ability to incorporate personality with social realities (Torres et al.,

2009). The process was dynamic because of a variety of forces or diversity (Torres et al., 2009). Diversity and identity were critical in social settings, and were congruent with Freud's identity definition: individuals tended to identify with his or her race, gender and ethnicity prior to any dyadic or intergroup interaction (Erickson, 1968; Tatum, 1997). An individual with a strong sense of self was considered socially competent, rare among Black males and challenging for Black Deaf males (Anderson & Miller, 2004; Crosby & Poussaint, 2007; Hrabowski III et al., 1998; McCaskill, 2005; Tatum, 1997).

Torres et al. (2009) suggested that daily interaction at school contributed to identity development because the school environment was a place where students explored the meaning of self and self-concept. An understanding of self was the foundation of self-esteem development (Erickson, 1968). Jambor & Elliott (2005) added that the quality of social life of the Deaf in regular education settings influenced his or her identity development.

A socially competent Black Deaf male student could have adapted in dyadic and intergroup interactions to reap educational benefits (Anderson & Miller, 2004; McCaskill, 2005). The Black Deaf male's inability to identify as Black or Deaf first interfered with his ability to reap educational benefits (Guyll et al., 2010). Instead of focusing on learning, the Black Deaf male was focused on trying to fit in (Anderson & Miller, 2004; McCaskill, 2005).

Social psychology and identity development. A sense of uniqueness and belonging was prerequisite to self-esteem development and group membership (Torres et al., 2009). The sense of uniqueness as in racial and ethnic or gender identification was congruent with Erickson's (1968) identity development theory. A sense of belonging was prerequisite to accepting oneself and successful dyadic and intergroup interaction and achievement (Erickson, 1968; Josselson, 1987). The sense of uniqueness and belonging helped individuals buffer psychological and sociological challenges in the environment (Josselson, 1987).

Josselson (1987) presented a definition of identity development relevant to the social psychological framework:

> Identity represents the intersection of the individual and society. In framing identity, the individual simultaneously joins the self to society and society to the self. As a result, identity comes to serve not only as a guardian of the integration and continuity of self-experience, but also as a mechanism for shared meaning-making that embeds the individual with those with whom life will be. (p. 12)

The implication of Josselson's (1987) definition for the Black Deaf male was that identity development was entwined in the complexity of societal and cultural demands. These demands challenged the Black Deaf male's ability to focus on one identity at a time. Josselson's (1987) definition also suggested a linear but dynamic process that began at birth. Black Deaf males were deprived of this process because of the dualism of culture and identity, which later created academic challenges that influenced their achievement— prophecy fulfilled (Guyll et al., 2010; Merton, 1948; Tauber, 1997).

Human and developmental ecology and identity development. The human and developmental ecology literature identified environmental complexities that could have influenced identity development related to mental ability, social skills, and academic achievement (Torres et al., 2009). The discussion used ecological metaphors to explain how personal characteristics interacted with the environment to promote or inhibit identity development (Renn, 2008). For example, a student tended to identify with his or her racial group to enhance his or her identity and fit in at school (Renn, 2008; Tatum, 1997). Fitting in, enhanced the student's ability to capitalize on campus services, which improved achievement (Tatum, 1997).

The Black Deaf male, then, had to fit in or identify with the Black hearing culture and the Deaf culture (Guyll et al., 2010). Each culture, Black and Deaf, had complex arrays of identity development requirements (Renn, 2008). For example, in Black hearing culture, identity development depended on skin color and the ability to speak and hear. Deaf culture identity development depended on the ability to use ASL to communicate (McCaskill, 2005). Black Deaf males' identification with the Black hearing culture and the Deaf culture were two simple examples of identity complexities in a global context. Society recognized ground rules and expectations on proper speaking, tone and body language use, but societal ground rules were different for the Black Deaf male who was depending on visual (ASL) communication.

The Black Deaf male's visual communication needs depended on his ability to learn and use ASL in the Deaf culture and his ability to learn and use English in the Black culture (McCaskill, 2005). For example, Bailes, Erting, Erting, and Thumann-Prezioso (2009) indicated that there were variations of ASL within the Deaf community similar to spoken accents that required adaptation. The variations created additional complexity in the use of ASL, which was the framework of the human and developmental ecology literature and was essential to the understanding of the Black Deaf male cultural and identity development (Renn, 2008; Torres et al., 2009).

Table 7 outlines the relationships between different identity development theoretical frameworks and self-fulfilling prophecy in Black Deaf males. The first column in Table 7 lists the four identity theoretical frameworks. The second and third columns compare the Black and Deaf or Deaf and Black identities depending on how an individual identified himself first (Guyll et al., 2010). The third column is the self-fulfilling prophecy implications for the Black Deaf male depending on identification.

Table 7

Cultural Dualism and Identity Development

Identity Theoretical Framework	Black or Deaf	SFP and Expectancy Implications
Psychological – cognitive development of "a healthy personality actively masters his environment, shows a certain unity of personality, and is able to perceive the world and himself correctly" (Erickson, 1968; p. 51).	Black: Identified as black based on color but Deaf – struggled with identity because black hearing heard and spoke with some advantages Deaf: Identified as Deaf but black – struggled with identity because White Deaf discriminated based on skin color	Black: Negative societal expectations since slavery. Deprivation to resources and opportunity to learn, which persisted and influenced achievement gap Deaf: Phonic and speaking expectations that hindered language acquisition, which led to one to three years achievement gap
Sociological – the ability to incorporate with social realities.	Black: Identity struggles because Black hearing had different social norms Deaf: Identity struggles because White Deaf identified Black Deaf as Black in social setting based on visual observation	Black: Teacher differential treatment the Golem effects, which often led to placement in special education classes due to misunderstanding of behavior Deaf: Teacher differential treatment the Golem effects, which often led to placement in special education classes due to inability to communicate
Social psychology – a sense of uniqueness and belonging, which enhanced self-esteem.	Black: Unique identity as Black Deaf but not unique as Black Deaf: Unique identity as Black Deaf but not unique are Deaf	Black: Teachers interpreted low self-esteem as laziness and lack of motivation to learn with differential treatment. Deaf: Teachers interpreted inability to speak as dumb and differential treatment persisted for that reason and often led to placement in special education classes
Human and development ecology – environmental complexity that influenced self and self in context.	Black: Experience societal biases and discrimination based on skin color, race, and ethnicity Deaf: Experience societal biases and discrimination based on inability to hear and speak and black	Black: Prophecy fulfilled with achievement gap disparities Deaf: Prophecy fulfilled with achievement gap disparities

Note. SFP = self-fulfilling prophecy

Gaps in the Literature

One of the existing gaps in the literature on factors that influenced the academic experience of Black Deaf male students was because this population had been historically overrepresented, culturally misunderstood, and placed in special education programs (Guyll et al., 2010; Lorsen & Orfield, 2002; McCaskill, 2005; U.S Department of Education, 2007). Poverty, drug abuse, unemployment, and socioeconomic were some of the most common risk factors discussed in research about the hearing African Americans' pedagogy (Cosby & Poussaint, 2007; Hrabowski III et al., 1998). The research failed to discuss or identify causes of the low achievements of Black Deaf male students (Williamson, 2007).

A more positive image and construction of identity were needed to fill research gaps about African American men that became the foundation to begin the Black Deaf male cultural dualism research (Guyll et al., 2010; McCaskill, 2005). However, the literature placed Golem-effect emphasis on inability and not enough Galatea effects on the abilities of today's Black man (Rubie-Davies et al., 2006). Harper and Nichols (2008) advised studies needed to analyze the perceptions of Black men beyond the community colleges and into 4-year colleges and universities. According to Tatum (1997), Blacks develop identity in adolescence and continue through adulthood, which creates an awareness of culture and racial identities.

Summary

An historical overview of the self-fulfilling prophecy derived from one of the three educational theories—functional, conflict, and symbolic interactionist—that led to the Thomas theorem and Merton's SFP theory was reviewed in this chapter. The literature about the Golem and Galatea effects of differential treatments, and how teacher expectations triggered the differential treatments, led to the fulfillment of the prophecies. The literature review was intended to show that the SFP phenomenon could have been responsible for the low academic achievement of the Black Deaf male student population.

A meticulous review of the literature regarding the SFP phenomenon was presented to compare and contrast three educational theories: functionalist, conflict, and symbolic interactionist. The literature reiterated the critical need for the symbolic interactionist theory micro-level observations to inform leadership and policy makers that the SFP phenomenon was only one factor in the discourse of the low achievement of minorities. A gap in the research about the SFP phenomenon relationship to the low achievement of minorities was identified. Chapter 3 incorporates the rationale for the study's design, method, and population. The next chapter contains an overview of the data collections process, data analysis and instrumentation, and concluded with the study's validity.

Chapter 3

Method

The purpose of this qualitative descriptive study was to explore the perceptions of a purposive sample of Black Deaf male students in the postsecondary setting in Washington D.C. to determine if the SFP theory contributed their pedagogic achievements. Specifically, this qualitative descriptive research study explored the SFP influence on the pedagogic achievement of Black Deaf male students and alumni. This chapter outlined the data collection method, and the *a posteriori* perceptions and *a priori* differential treatments from the population of this study to determine if the self-fulfilling prophecy theory contributed to their pedagogic achievements.

The population in this study included Black Deaf male postsecondary undergraduates and graduates who matriculated and maintained an average cumulative GPA between 2.0 and 4.0 at the time of graduation. The GPA indicator was important because it was a standard used to measure academic success in the postsecondary setting (Sanchez & Sital, 2010). According to Oseguera (2005) minority postsecondary students who went on to graduate completed undergraduate coursework with a C grade or better, led to a GPA of between 2.0 and 4.0. The Black Deaf male was a minority population that had the lowest graduation rate and this study aimed to understand if the SFP was a factor that was influencing their academics (Gallaudet Enrollment Reports, 2000-2006).

Research Method and Design Appropriateness

This study employed a qualitative descriptive research method to address the research problem and purpose. A qualitative descriptive method was utilized to collect the data, explain the data collections process, the instrument used to collect the data, the sample size, and the method for analyzing the research design. A qualitative descriptive method was appropriate for this study to allow subjects an opportunity to express perceptions of their pedagogic.

According to Castellan (2010), the qualitative approach permits the researcher to interpret and summarize the perceptions. The qualitative method was congruent with the symbolic interactionist theory about the exploration of the central phenomena (Smit & Fritz, 2008). The descriptive inquiry allowed the subjects to express their unnoticed experiences that were undoubted because they were the primary source (Campbell & Roden, 2010). The source of knowledge was that real and ideal content experience dwelt in our memory (Neuman, 2006).

This qualitative descriptive design was used to survey the study population to capture detailed information about some potential factors within higher education setting that affected their achievement (Neuman, 2006). According to Creswell (2005), a qualitative descriptive research design was appropriate for this study because qualitative research explored the perceptions of the study population classroom experience. The perceptions of the Black Deaf male student's pedagogic experience were also explored in this probe. The inquiry provided an overview of the Black Deaf male student's cultural dualism identity challenges that might have influenced his ability to navigate the higher education academic environment.

Neuman (2006) expanded qualitative researchers generalized on themes, ideas, and concepts and quantitative analysis were based on simple nominal variables and non-variable concepts. Quantitative research placed "an emphasis on collecting and analyzing information in the form of numbers" (Creswell, 2005, p. 41). The quantitative analysis of numbers was the type of inquiry that omitted descriptions and interpretations of the qualitative research (Creswell, 2005).

Creswell (2005) indicated that the quantitative approach was inappropriate for descriptive studies because of its deductive and logical nature. The quantitative and mixed-methods research designs incorporated hypotheses, theories, and variables, and were mathematically driven to enhance validity—which was not the intent of this research (Creswell, 2005; Meyer & Munson, 2005). According to Creswell (2005), "Quantitative research is deductive, and research questions and hypothesis do not change during the study" (p. 133).

Neuman (2006) furthered that an ethnographic research approach allowed the researcher to observe subjects and participated in the present time in the researcher's home culture. The ethnographic method, which seemed inappropriate for this study, required extensive planning and time in which the researcher immersed in the natural setting to observe the participants in the study to gain detailed insights about the cultural experiences of the participants (Campbell & Roden, 2010). Therefore, an ethnographic design would not accomplish the research goal in this study. Literature on Deaf and Hard of Hearing postsecondary experiences typically categorized the Black Deaf male population under generic and inclusive labels such as special education, mentally retarded, children with hearing loss, Deaf and Hard of Hearing and children with hearing impairment (Hrabowski III et al., 1998; Richardson et al., 2010; Skiba et al., 2008; U.S. Department of Education, 2007, 2010). Insufficient research was available that focused on American Black Deaf male students' postsecondary achievements.

An open-ended survey was administered to 10 Black Deaf male students and 10 alumni. The intent of the survey was to determine how the self-fulfilling prophecy theory contributed to their scholastic outcomes. The results were intended to assist researchers, faculty, staff, and university administrators in planning and implementing intervention and retention programs to improve the achievement gap. Campbell and Roden (2010) stated that the qualitative research design was appropriate for situations in which the outcomes could influence the well being of the students in the academic environment. To that end, the qualitative descriptive design was appropriate for this study to explore the *a posteriori* perceptions of differential treatments and culturally dualistic experiences of Black Deaf male students in postsecondary settings.

Population

The population of this study was a purposive sample (Creswell, 2005) of Black Deaf male students with the lowest graduation rates compared to Black hearing male students (Gallaudet University Enrollment Reports, 2000-2006; JBHE, 2007). This qualitative descriptive study purported to examine the influence of the SFP on Black Deaf male students at a university in Washington, D.C. Creswell (2005) defined population as "a group of individuals who have the same characteristics" (p. 145). Postsecondary Black Deaf male students who graduated with a GPA between 2.0 and 4.0 were surveyed to understand the descriptive relationship between the SFP and academic achievements. Analysis of the themes should have generated awareness among Black Deaf male students, faculty and staff and education leadership about the widening achievement gap between this population and the general population.

Sample Frame

A critical sample size (Creswell, 2005) of Black Deaf males at a postsecondary setting in Washington, D.C. was selected for the current study because this population had the lowest postsecondary graduation rates at the university (Gallaudet University Enrollment Reports, 2000-2006). The goal of the qualitative descriptive research was to understand the Black Deaf male student's pedagogic perceptions in the classroom. An assumption was made that Black Deaf male postsecondary students who graduated with a GPA between 2.0 and 4.0 participated in this study.

Informed Consent

The informed consent document was intended to preserve the autonomy of the research participants by providing information about the research process, and assured participants that they were volunteers who could have decided not to participate (Eyler & Jeste, 2006). According to Eyler and Jeste (2006), researchers "provide as outline of areas that are in need of future studies in order to reach the ultimate goal of preserving as much autonomy as possible in at-risk populations, while still achieving valuable research and treatment goals" (p. 533). All research participants received an informed consent letter that explained the purpose of the study and the influence of the self-fulfilling prophecy on the Black Deaf male students' academic experience (see Appendix A).

A brief introduction of the study, accompanied by an overview of the significance and intended contributions, were in the informed consent letter. The letter shared the importance of anonymity and confidentiality should the study be published. The consent form (see Appendix A) was included in the survey questions and sent via United States Postal Service to be signed and returned with the completed survey.

Confidentiality

All of the research documents were kept confidential. The researcher administered the surveys, collected, and analyzed the data. All research data, including informed consent forms, interview transcripts, notes, data analysis, and electronic files, were kept in locked storage at least three years from the dissertation and approval dates. All materials were destroyed at the end of the 3-year holding period unless the requirements for holding the information changed. The information and material were destroyed according to methods for destroying sensitive, personal information, such as cross-shredding paper materials and erasing, overwriting, or physically destroying any electronic media.

Geographic Location

The research study focused on Black Deaf male students currently enrolled at or already graduated from an institution of higher education in Washington, D.C. The geographical locations of the study participants were extended outside of Washington, D.C., given how some participants outside of the institution's vicinity. The data collection locations were at the participants' convenience.

Instrumentation

The focus of this qualitative descriptive study was to disseminate an open-ended survey to Black Deaf male student undergraduates at a university in Washington, D.C. and graduates around the United States. The survey was sent to participants via the United States Postal Service with a stamped, self-addressed envelope. The intent was to identify SFP influences on the academic achievements of the participants in this study.

The open-ended survey questions (see Appendix B) were derived from Merton's (1948), and Tauber's (1997) SFP definition and the two aforementioned research questions.

Data Collection

A qualitative survey was the primary data collection source. The survey consisted of open-ended questions derived from the two research questions. Participants were recruited by using several means. An advertisement was placed in the Gallaudet University alumni newsletter, the National Black Deaf Advocates (NBDA) homepage, and the university daily digest newspaper online (Appendix G). Surveys were mailed to respondents via the United States Postal Service. Mailed surveys included a package that contains a letter of consent to participate in the study, a permission form that explains the research, and a confidentiality agreement form.

A recruitment booth was also used to recruit both undergraduates and alumni during a homecoming event at the university. A recruitment flyer (Appendix E) was posted around the university bulletin boards, in the dormitory, student cafeteria, and the daily digest news to recruit undergraduate subjects. Some undergraduates elected to complete the survey at the recruitment booth during Homecoming.

Pilot Study

Prior to the beginning of the study, a pilot study was conducted by the researcher with five participants, excluded from the purposive sample of participants, to help validation of the data collection instrument (see Appendix B). The participants were recruited using the recruitment flyer (Appendix E). Participant responses remained anonymous to ensure confidentiality. The survey provided a means to identify SFP themes and patterns by collecting responses to open-ended questions. The research questions drove the data collection process for this qualitative descriptive research study and expanded upon existing literature concerning rationale for Black Deaf male students' academic achievement.

Validity

Internal validity. Internal validity is concerned with the study design that may affect the outcome (Creswell, 2005; Neuman, 2006). In this study, the data collection instrument was pretested with five participants to ensure that the instrument addressed the purpose statement, answered the research questions, and were understood by subjects. The pretest participants were not included in the purposive sample to validate the data collection instrument.

External validity. According to Kuper, Lingard, & Levinson (2008), "The sample should be broad enough to capture the many facets of a phenomenon, and limitations to the sample should be clearly justified" (p. 687). The responses from the pilot test participants indicated comparable responses to some of the survey questions. Therefore, the survey instrument satisfied the requirements for external validity.

Data Analysis

The data was analyzed using Microsoft Excel and Word software for SFP themes such as teacher expectations, differential treatment, behavior and achievement verbalization, achievement consistency, and time (Merton, 1948; Tauber, 1997). The open-ended survey questions should have revealed the opinions and perceptions of the SFP phenomena among Black Deaf males. According to Creswell (2005), "The coding process is a qualitative research process in which the researcher makes sense out of text data, divides it into text or image segments, labels the segments, examines codes for overlaps and redundancy, and collapse these codes into themes" (p. 624). Microsoft Excel and Word software were used to code the data for the SFP themes.

Procedures

Content analysis. A content analysis methodology was used to analyze the data. According to Krippendorff (2013) "Content analysis is a research technique for making replicable and valid inferences from texts (or other meaningful matter) to the context of their use" (p. 24). Stepchenkova, Kirilenko, and Morrison (2009) indicated content analysis was used to analyze textual data from open-ended questions "to discern meaning from this wealth of textual material" (p. 467).

Content analysis in qualitative descriptive studies helped the researcher to analyze text that described meaning of the study participants' experiences (Jackson, Drummond, & Camara, 2007). Gubrium and Holstein (1997), as cited in Jackson et al. (2007), indicated,

> Essentially, qualitative content analysis involves interpreting, theorizing, or making sense of data by first breaking it down into segments that can be categorized and coded, and then establishing a pattern for the entire data set by relating the categories to one another. (p. 24)

The content analysis process involved a coding process where the researcher categorized text data into fragments to establish patterns.

Hsieh and Shannon (2005) suggested two strategies that a researcher could use in content analysis to code data depending on the research question. The first strategy was for the researcher to read and highlight text that represented the theme and then code the highlighted text using predetermined codes. The second strategy was "to begin coding immediately with the predetermined codes" (Hsieh & Shannon, 2005, p. 1282).

The researcher used the second strategy to code the responses to the open-end survey of this research ((Hsieh & Shannon, 2005). This approached involved the use of inductive reasoning. Inductive reasoning allowed the research to narrow detailed and complex text data into general codes and themes (Creswell, 2009). White and Marsh (2006) elaborated that content analysis inferences allowed the researcher to use "analytical constructs" (p. 27) to make inferences about the text.

The process of making inferences about the data consisted of generalizing text data, coding, textual descriptions, categorizing, and creating themes. Upon receipt of the open-ended surveys, data were entered into Microsoft Excel for further analysis. The goal of the content analysis was to infer parallel themes to predetermined SFP themes, teacher expectations, differential treatment, behavior and achievement verbalization, achievement consistency, and time (Tauber, 1997).

Coding. Alphanumeric codes were manually assigned to participants. The following coding scheme was used to identify undergraduates and alumni. The letters UG and numbers 10 through 20 were used to identify undergraduate respondents. Alumni letters were AL followed by the numbers 10 through 20. The following represented the undergraduate coding process: UG10, UG11, UG12, UG13, UG14, UG15, UG16, UG17, UG18, UG19, and UG20 respectively. Similarly, alumni codes were AL10, AL11, AL12, AL13, AL14, AL15, AL16, AL17, AL18, AL19, and AL20.

Coding process. The responses were entered into Microsoft Excel. The research questions (RQ1 – RQ15) were entered to correspond with textual responses from undergraduates (UG10 – UG20) and graduates (AL10 – AL20). Textual responses and comments from the open-ended survey were color coded to begin grouping, segmenting, and categorizing them into chunks (Trochim & Donnelly, 2008).

Trochim and Donnelly (2008) called this process "unitizing, the process of breaking continuous text into separate units that can subsequently be coded" (p. 151). Instances where there were no comments were not included. Irrelevant textual responses and comments were eliminated or not included.

The reduced color-coded textual responses were extracted and placed into a new Microsoft Excel worksheet for further analysis and coding. The unitization allowed the researcher to eliminate all personal pronouns from the textual responses. The reduced text was separated by a semicolon and moved into a new Microsoft Excel worksheet. The reduced text was further reduced to allow the researcher to make inferences to create new meanings that close related to the predetermined sub-themes.

The next step involved transfer of predetermined sub-theme units to create themes specific for this study (Table 8). Table 8 illustrated how content analysis was used to unitize text responses, create sub-themes, code, and to generate themes and textual descriptions. The content analysis process was used to analyze textual response of undergraduate and graduates.

Table 8

Sample content analysis

RQ1	UG1	Content analysis	Inferred meanings	Possible pre-determined sub-themes	Themes	Textual description
What is your perception of your college professor's expectations of your academic performance?	My professor set high expectations of my academic performance	Set high expectations; academic performance	Expectancy means	Success Failure Neutral	High, low, No expectations	Strategies used to form expectations
Comment	Because it was suppose to learn things we never learn before	College; learn things; never learn before	Expectancy tools	Achievement Knowledge Exposure	Self-expectations; Syllabic expectations; Reminders	Realization of the SFP, or resistant to the SFP

Notes: RQ = research question; UG = undergraduate

Summary

The method for collecting, analyzing, and interpreting descriptive research data to explore the perceptions of the study population pedagogic was presented in this chapter. The data was entered into Microsoft Excel and Word to extrapolate parallel themes to predetermined SFP themes such as teacher expectations, differential treatment, behavior and achievement verbalization, achievement consistency, and time (Tauber, 1997). Finally, this chapter outlined a qualitative research design that was intended to reveal outcomes that influenced the Black Deaf male student's insights about his academic environment (Castellan, 2010).

Chapter 4 outlines the research findings and heightened leadership awareness about segregating data reporting structures for minorities and individuals with disabilities. A segregated data reporting structure in this context was intended to localize causes for low achievements among Black Deaf male students. The research outcome highlighted coping strategies for those students in navigating the postsecondary setting. Substantial strategic information could have been incorporated into faculty development programs to enhance mentoring skills, and to increase faculty awareness of potential unintentional biases the Black Deaf male student's academic achievements experienced in simple descriptive terms.

Chapter 4

Analysis and Results

The purpose of this qualitative descriptive study was to explore the perceptions of a purposive sample of Black Deaf male students in postsecondary setting in Washington, D.C., to determine if the SFP theory contributed to their pedagogic achievements. The specific problem was that the Black Deaf male student's perception of teacher expectations about his academic abilities and the teacher's expectations were influencing his overall academic achievement. The research outcomes highlighted coping strategies in postsecondary setting for Black Deaf male students. The intention of this study was to generate awareness to educate advocates, policymakers, leadership, educational leadership, and teachers.

This chapter presents an inquiry of the data and research outcomes attained from the qualitative survey, describes the data collection process, and the SFP thematic outcomes. The results included survey responses and comments from 10 undergraduates (UG) and 10 Black Deaf male alumni (AL). Microsoft Excel and Word software were used to analyze the survey responses. The objective was to categorize the teacher's expectations, differential treatment, behavior and achievement verbalization, achievement consistency, and time SFP themes (Merton, 1948; Tauber, 1997).

Two research questions that guided this study were: (R1) how do Black Deaf male students perceive a teacher's expectations of their academic performances in postsecondary institutions, and (R2) how do Black Deaf male students perceive a teacher's expectations that influence their achievements? The R1 investigated the SFP themes as factors that influenced the Black Deaf male students' postsecondary experiences. The R2 explored how expectations influenced academic achievements among Black Deaf males. The general problem was that Black Deaf male students experienced Black and Deaf cultural dualism, ethnicity challenges, and overrepresentation in special education programs. These experiences could have been susceptible to the SFP phenomena and low graduation rates.

Researching Black Deaf male students' perceptions in postsecondary setting identified coping strategies for the students. This research is a topic that is suggested as a potential professional development topic for faculty, mentors, and postsecondary administration at higher education institutions. This inquiry has added data that explored the general problem and supplemented SFP research.

Pilot Study

A pilot study was conducted with participants who completed the survey and provided feedback. The pilot study participants were informed face-to-face that after they completed the survey using ASL, their responses would not be included in the final study. The researcher explained to the five pilot participants that their feedback and critique would be used to improve the survey instrument. At the end of the pilot study, the participants stated that they understood the survey and reported that it was easy to complete. No changes were made to the original survey based on the participants' feedback.

Data Collection

The participants of this study were recruited in several ways. A flyer was posted on the Gallaudet University daily digest newspaper online (Appendix G). The flyer was also sent via the Gallaudet University alumni e-mailed newsletter, and posted on the homepage of National Black Deaf Advocates (NBDA) (Appendix I).

Black Deaf male alumni participants responded at different times via e-mail, expressing willingness to be a survey participant. The survey was mailed to the participants using the United States Postal Service and included a self-addressed return envelope. Most alumni returned the completed survey within a week. To ensure confidentiality, alumni names and addresses on the self-addressed envelopes were shredded.

Alumni were compensated via mail with an American Express gift card for completing the survey. A recruitment booth was also set up during Gallaudet University's homecoming and at a Northern Virginia basketball tournament to recruit Black Deaf male alumni who graduated between 2002 and 2009 (Appendix I). A recruitment poster was used to recruit Black Deaf undergraduate students (Appendix G). All of the undergraduates completed the survey at the recruitment booths. The alumni and undergraduate respondents were coded as AL10 to AL20 and UG10 to UG20 to maintain confidentiality.

All research data, including informed consent forms, interview transcripts, notes, data analysis, and electronic files, will be kept in locked storage at least three years from the dissertation and approval dates. The information and material will be destroyed according to methods for destroying sensitive, personal information, such as cross-shredding paper materials and erasing, overwriting, or physically destroying any electronic media.

Demographics

The population of this study included 10 Black Deaf male undergraduates and 10 alumni. Alumni graduated between 2002 and 2009. The population of this study was expected to have maintained a GPA between 2.0 and 4.0 (Oseguera, 2005). The population of this study was from the United States of America. Foreign-born Black Deaf males were excluded from this study because American-born Black males were found to have the lowest graduation rates (Gallaudet University Enrollment Report 2000–2006; JBHE, 2007; U.S. Department of Education, 2009). Each participant spent approximately 20 to 30 minutes completing the survey.

Presentation of Data Analysis

Content analysis was used to analyze and code the data.

> The coding process is a qualitative research process in which the researcher makes sense out of text data, divides it into text or image segments, labels the segments, examines codes for overlaps and redundancy, and collapses these codes into themes. (Creswell, 2005, p. 624)

The two research questions were clustered with analogous survey questions to begin the SFP thematic coding process (Tables 15–19, Appendix H). Microsoft Excel and Word software were used to create textual units for this analysis.

Table 15 presents the R1 with the SFP step 1 (teacher forms expectations), and three corresponding survey questions. Table 16 offers the R2 with the SFP step 2 (based on these expectations, the teacher acted in a differential manner), and three matching survey questions. Table 17 reviews the R2 with the SFP step 3 (the teacher's treatment told each student what behaviors and achievement the teacher expected), and three equivalent survey questions. Table 18 constructs the R2 with the SFP step 4 (if the treatment is consistent over time, and if the student did not actively resist, it tended to shape his or her behavior and achievement), and four comparable survey questions. Table 19 shows the R2 with the final SFP step (with time, the student's behavior and achievement conformed more closely to that expected of him or her), and three analogous survey questions.

The survey questions were grouped to match with participant and comments (Tables 20–39, Appendix H). Tables 20–23 show survey questions 1, 2, and 3, participants, remarks, and statistics associated to the SFP step 1. The textual responses were entered into Microsoft Excel to create textual units for further analysis.

The reduced text from the unitization process was transferred to Microsoft Word to create inferred meanings. The meanings were expanded to create sub-themes. The sub-themes analysis of this data yielded three specific themes for this study related to the first SFP theme, teacher forms expectations (Table 9 and 15). This content analysis process was used to analyze the remaining textual data sets for this study.

Tables 24–27 (Appendix H) clusters survey questions 4, 5, and 6, participants, statements, and data connected to the SFP step 2, which generated three themes (Table 11). Tables 28–30 (Appendix H) groups survey questions 7 and 8, participants, interpretations, and records correlated to the SFP step 3, producing three themes (Table 12). Tables 31–35 assemble survey questions 9 through 12; participants, annotations, and indicators related to the SFP step 4, which formed three themes (Table 13).

Tables 36–39 bundle the final three survey questions, participants, comments, and numbers related to the final SFP step, conformity, which generated three themes (Table

14). Clustering the data allowed the researcher to make sense of textual responses. The textual responses were reduced to create inferences, which were segmented into sub-groups that led to the identification of emergent themes (Tables 9). Textual and structural descriptions were constructed to show the meaning of the perceptions for the study participants (Table 9).

Findings

The survey obtained Black Deaf male students' and alumni responses and comments on their perceptions during dyadic interactions with their teachers in classrooms in a postsecondary setting. The goal was to determine if the SFP influenced their classroom achievement or lack thereof. The data comprised responses of the five SFP steps, teacher expectations, differential treatment, behavior and achievement verbalization, achievement consistency, and time.

The responses were analyzed in Microsoft (MS) Excel and Word software for emerging themes. The researcher grouped the R1, R2, The five SFP steps, and corresponding survey questions (Table 15–19, Appendix H). The survey questions, UG responses, AL response, and comments were clustered to correspond with R1 and R2, corresponding SQ, responses, and comments into MS Word (Table 20–39, Appendix H). The textual responses and comments were transferred into Microsoft Excel to create textual units for further analysis.

A six-step content analysis process was used to analyze the data in MS Excel and Word software. The first step highlighted the textual responses by eliminating all personal pronouns in MS Excel. The second step involved transfer of the highlighted text to a new Excel worksheet to create individual units (Tables 23, 27, 30, 35, and 39,

Appendix H). The third step transferred the unitized text to MS Word to create inferred meanings. The fourth step had the meanings expanded to create possible predetermined sub-themes (Table 8). The fifth step counted the sub-themes using the COUNT formula in MS Excel to group invariant constituents to indicate the distribution frequencies to create emergent themes (Table 9, left column) specifically for this study. The sixth step had textual descriptions inductively developed for the emergent themes that corresponded with each of the five SFP steps (Table 9, right column).

Table 9

Emerging Themes and Textual Description

Emergent Themes	Textual Description
Syllabic expectations Self-expectations No-high-low expectations	Strategies used to form expectations
Eye contact-acknowledgement Attitudinal indifference Public praise-positive-negative comments	Cues such as body language and other props used to reinforce differential treatments
Personalized one-on-one attention Pop quiz reminders Office hours-after class counseling	Modes of communication used to reinforce behavior and achievement expectations
Team assignments Verbal-written-positive-negative feedback Private-public-verbal-written reinforcements	Tactics used to maintain differential treatment consistency
Probing Reminders Self-motivation	Realization of the SFP or resistant to the SFP

Themes

The themes emerged from the analysis using content analysis methodology in Microsoft Excel and Word software. The next section discusses the emergent themes, textual descriptions, and descriptive statistics. The first step in the SFP was the formation of expectations. Three themes emerged from the analysis of the descriptive statistics about how the teacher formed expectations (Tables 10).

Table 10

Formed Expectations Themes

Emergent Themes	Textual Description
Syllabic expectations	Strategies used to form expectations
Self-expectations	
No-high-low expectations	

Syllabic expectations. The syllabic expectation theme indicated that teachers used the course syllabus to form expectations (Table 10). This theme originated from survey questions 1, 2, and 3. The first survey question explored participants' perception of how teachers set expectations. The study identified 7 out of 10 AL and 4 out of 10 UG who indicated that teachers set expectations during class and used the course syllabus to set expectations (Table 23). Some comments included "Syllabus," by UG12, "Professors would explain/hold their expectations during class. I felt that apply to everyone," by AL13, and "Expectations were on just about every syllabus. However, when it came to grading[,] the syllabus & expectations weren't always followed," by AL10.

The second survey question explored participants' perception of how teacher expectations influenced their classroom performance in a positive way. This survey question was intended to solicit participants' perception of additional strategies that teachers used to set and hold expectations. The study classified 6 out of 10 UG who specified that teachers used homework; a requirement in the syllabus to influenced their classroom performance in a positive way.

The study categorized 4 out of 10 AL who stipulated that teachers used public praise to influence their classroom performance in a positive way. The study also identified 2 out of 10 of both UG and AL who specifically stated that teachers used the course syllabus to influence their classroom performance in a positive way. UG10 said, "The professor told the class about his or her expectations and thoroughly discussed the syllabus[,] and the professor encouraged my classmates and me to take advantage of his or her office hours," and UG12 commented, "That has always helped me perform better. A [p]rofessor who does not show favoritism." AL13 added, "Professor treat[s] their students equally; [sic] [I] will feel included and not singl[ed] out," and AL17 said, "She has high expectations for us and want to share our work."

The third question sought to identify participants' perceptions of how a set of expectations influenced their classroom performance in a negative way. The intent of this question was to solicit response consistency from the participants about the formed expectations with respect to survey questions one and two. The study identified 2 out of 10 from both UG and AL who indicated that teachers did not set expectations. The study also identified 4 out of 10 AL who did not answer. UG14 said, "I like it when professor's [sic] are up front about expectations," and UG15 took responsibility: "Because sometimes I don't realize to turn in my homework in the class that I have homework..." AL comments were congruent with UG. AL12 indicated, "None of the response[s] apply to me. My negative classroom performance is because I didn't do my best," and AL14 stated, "I felt that [the] professor expected me to fix the problem on my own without asking for assistance." The low response to this survey question validated survey questions one and two in that teachers used the course syllabus to form positive expectations.

Self-expectations. The self-expectation theme inferred that some of the participants formed expectations, an indication that some participants resisted teacher expectations or did not take teacher expectations into account (Table 10). The study found 14 AL instances and 3 UG invariant constituents who set their own expectations (Tables 20–39, Appendix H). Participants with self-expectation themes viewed their education as a self-responsibility.

AL17 said, "I chose [to] set my own expectation of my academic performance because I can't expect my professor's expectation of my [performance]. Professors teach many students [and] I can't rely [on them]. I have my own academic goal, [it] is to complete my college degree," and AL16 added,

> Some of my professors met with me after class or met at his or her office hours to discuss about my academic performance. I had set my own expectation and cared about my academic[s] so if I didn't do well I met with my professor asked for advice or feedback as so what I need to improve.

No/low/high/unclear expectations. The no-low-high-unclear expectations theme extrapolated that teachers either set no expectations, set expectations that weren't high or low, or set expectations that were not clear. The data analysis classified 2 out of 10 UG and 2 out of 10 AL who said expectation were not set. In addition, 2 out of 10 UG and 6 out of 10 AL mentioned that expectations were set but they were neither high nor low (Tables 20–39, Appendix H). The participants of this study had a variety of perceptions. An UG and 3 AL held that expectations were unclear. Comments included, "Professor just did not care, it seemed," (UG11) and "Nothing" from UG12. Some commentaries from alumni participants included "No set expectations of a class; clueless" (AL13).

The next part discussed the second step in the SFP: differential treatment themes (Table 11). Three themes were developed from the three-survey questions addendum with observations. The intent was to explore participants' perceptions of teachers' differential treatments that communicated expectations with respect to non-verbal communication.

Table 11

Differential Treatment Themes

Emergent Themes	Textual Description
Eye contact-acknowledgement	Cues such as body language and actions used to reinforce differential treatments
Attitudinal indifference	
Public praise-positive-negative comments	

Eye contact/acknowledgement. This theme was indication of a differential treatment that teachers used to reinforce expectations. The study identified 6 out of 10 UG participants who stated teachers made "eye contact with them to communicate expectations." UG16 observed, "Because communication is key to avoid the forgettable." The study classified 4 out of 10 UG participants who affirmed that teachers acknowledged them in and outside the classroom. The acknowledgement was a form of non-verbal cues that teachers used to communicate expectations. UG11 said, "This is related to the high expectations thing when I was not performing well. The professor automatically knew something was wrong." UG14 added, "Sharing information that would help my academic environment in and out of class."

The study found 4 out of 10 AL participants specified that the teachers' eye contact was a form of non-verbal cue to strengthen expectations. AL15 specified, "I felt that [the] professor wanted to see me to do well in the class for the whole semester if I wish to meet the expectations." AL19 stated, "When I need her, she always made eye contact to make sure I [paid] attention."

Attitudinal indifference. This theme developed from invariant constituents where the study participants perceived attitudinal indifference in the teacher's non-verbal communications to formed expectations. Participants perceived that a teacher's attitudinal indifference led to poor performance. The study classified nine invariant constituents that UG perceived teachers' negative attitudinal indifference. UG10 mentioned, "There was the one who would do that. So [I] hated it" and "Had one professor who was very apathetic. I went through some really tough times (death etc.) seem[ed] like she did not care." UG13, however, wrote, "Never had a professor do that."

The study categorized 10 invariant constituents (AL) who perceived teachers' negative attitudinal indifference. AL10 observed, "I could easily read the majority of my professors whom did not know me well. They basically target away from me while directing most of the attention to the majority of my White peers. I was somewhat invisible," and "I felt even at the graduate level when I didn't do something the way they wanted it done it was almost as if I might as well died. They had limited office hours and was tough to meet them and I didn't feel comfortable asking for help after the first meeting because of their nonchalant attitude." AL12 commented, "While expectations were established in class, I don't recall being praised for my good work to a point where everyone in class would acknowledge it so it wasn't clear" and "While everyone's work may vary to some extent, most of my professors provided general comments to the entire class without reaching out to further praise those like me who did better."

Public praise – positive/negative comments. This theme derived from participants' perception that in addition to non-verbal communication, teachers used other methods to reinforce expectations. The study identified 15 UG invariant constituents related to this theme. UG11 remarked, "I think what helped was the fact that my professors noticed the shyness that I have. They know what I am capable of but I hold myself back. Some of these professors have really helped me open up." UG13 noted, "He is being more positive [with] me when I made mistakes and he is always same person to me."

The study classified 13 AL invariant constituents associated with this theme. AL13 stated, "Verbal praises to everyone from the professor may have positively influenced my classroom performance but it's really my hard work that makes a difference." AL14 noted, "Professors were impressed [and] praised when I provided my contribution to share with peers in classroom."

The next segment focused on the third SFP step: modes of communication used to send a message to participants about behavior and achievement expectations. The intent was to solicit participants' perception of behavior and achievement expectations. Responses indicated that participants perceived that teachers used different modes of communication behavior and achievement expectations. Three themes emerged from the study (Table 12).

Personalized one-on-one attention. The study identified 4 out of 10 UG and 3 out of 10 AL. UG12 commented, "One-on-one attention save my time." AL16 added, "I encouraged myself to meet one-on-one with my professor in order to get better understanding and improve my academic performance."

Table 12

Modes of Communication Themes

Emergent Themes	Textual Description
Personalized one-on-one attention	Modes of communication used to reinforce behavior and achievement expectations
Pop-quizzes reminders	
Office hours-after class counseling	

Pop-quiz reminders. The study classified 7 out of 10 UG and 6 out of 10 AL. UG10 mentioned, "To remind me I can do this. Helped me slow down and focus," and UG17 wrote, "Because it helps [remind me about] the homework… through syllabus." AL10 said, "These quizzes determined how much information I was actually learning and remembering. Listening skills [were] better than I expected," and AL13 stated, "Constant reminders to the students of one's expectations."

Office hours/after class counseling. The study categorized 16 UG invariant constituents. UG11 stated, "My professor met with me during office hours to make sure I was clear about his or her expectations of me," and UG13 said, "Often times I could request to meet with the professor, or he or she would remind me of his/her office hours. Then we could talk about my subpar performance and how it could improve." AL14 indicated, "Communication through email [and] in the office hours," and AL16 stated,

> Some of my professors met with me after class or met at his or her office hours to discuss about my academic performance. I had set my own expectation and cared about my academic so if I didn't do well I met with my professor asked for advice or feedback as to what I need to improve.

The next subdivision discussed the fourth SFP step: consistent treatment over time to shape behavior and achievement to expectation. The intent was to explore participants who did not actively resist expectations. Replies indicated that participants did not actively resist expectations. The exploration identified three themes (Table 13).

Team assignments. The study identified 6 out of 10 UG and 4 out of 10 AL. UG13 mentioned, "He want[ed] to make sure that I participate[d] a lot... he will give more credit," and UG15 commented, "Because participat[ing] with classmate[s] is key." AL14 stated, "Some peers had different cultural backgrounds [that] challenged me to accept [and] work better with peers[, it] helped me [become] fully aware in future jobs after graduation," and AL16 said, "It [is] base[d] on what type of course that I took. Some require[d] my hard work because my teammates [didn't] know how to make it work. Some[times] I learned from my teammate[s more] than what I learn[ed] from teachers."

Table 13

Consistency Themes

Emergent Themes	Textual Description
Team assignments	Tactics used to maintain differential treatment consistency
Verbal-written-positive-negative feedback	
Private-public-verbal-written reinforcements	

Verbal/written – positive/negative feedback. The study identified 12 UG invariant constituents and 13 AL invariant constituents. UG10 commented, "They [are] always giving me feedback to make [it so] I can get a better grade," and UG17 indicated, "Because feedback is always helpful so I can do better next time." AL10 stated, "In some of my papers my professor praised my work. At times when I needed feedback the most to assure I was in the right track my professor did this," and AL13 specified, "Professors give feedback for everyone. And if [I'm] struggling, [they] make additional comments."

Private/public – verbal/written reinforcements. The study identified 5 out of 10 UG and 4 out of 10 AL. UG10 mentioned, "They comment something if I do great," and UG12 detailed, "My professor would write profound statements on my papers if I did really well or surpassed her/his expectations." AL13 stated, "The[y] would write comments on my paper like 'good point' or 'analysis'," and AL17 wrote,

> Some teacher[s] push me really hard to improve my work quality to succeed my level where I can produce in real world. Most teacher[s] will just leave me alone as I am the best student in class that don't need any help and help other students more than me.

The next section discusses the final step in the SFP theory: that the student eventually moves closely to conform to the teacher's *a priori* expectation if he or she doesn't actively resist the initially formed expectations from SFP step one. The intent was to explore participants' perception of the SFP Galatea or Golem effects. Responses indicated that participants perceived Galatea effects SFP in the classroom. Three themes emerged from the investigation (Table 14).

Table 14

SFP Themes

Emergent Themes	Textual Description
Probing	Realization of the SFP or resistant to the SFP
Reminders	
Self-motivation	

Probing. Probing was one way a teacher established high and low expectations for the students. The data classified 4 out of 10 UG and 7 out of 10 AL. UG12 observed, "This kept us on our toes," and UG15 stated, "Helps to keep information fresh in your mind." AL10 noted, "Professors always tended to want to know what I think first before any other students in the class," and AL13 added, "This tactics of calling me to respond to questions I didn't volunteer to answer helped prepare me to make sure I understand my reading materials before I come to class." The participants had the perception that their teachers used probing to confirm the Galatea effects SFP.

Reminders. The reminders theme was another approach a teacher could have used to reinforce formed expectations with respect to the SFP step one. The data analysis yielded 6 out of 10 UG and 5 out of 10 AL. UG10 mentioned, "Sometimes this was done to motivate others to excel also" and UG11 noted,

> I was at the point where I could have given up but my teacher did not give up on me. I allowed my own personal issues to get in the way of my academic performance. She saw that and helped me focus on my work.

AL13 commented, "Constant reminders to the students of one's expectations" and AL14 added, "'Good job' 'Excellent' were very positive from [the] professor." The participants perceived that teachers used this theme to validate Galatea effects SFP.

Self-motivation. The self-motivation theme was a resistance to teacher expectations, which indicated that the participants of this study might have resisted the teacher's expectations. The study identified 3 UG and 16 AL invariant constituents. UG12 commented, "I paid [for] the course so I have to do well in school. My responsibility, my choice, my decision," and UG16 said, "Encouragement from teachers are nice but self motivation is better." AL14 noted, "During Gallaudet years, I set my own expectations to achieve my academic performances regardless of my professors' expectations because I had goals to complete [and] graduate" and added, "I follow[ed] what [was] needed to achieve my academic goals."

Summary

The intent of this study was to explore if the SFP theory contributed to the pedagogic achievements of a purposive sample of Black Deaf male students in a Washington, D.C. postsecondary setting. This study explored Black Deaf male students' pedagogic in higher education. The population of this study was surveyed to determine how the SFP phenomenon influenced or did not influence their academic experiences. The two research questions, 15 survey questions, and commentaries that guided this exploration were outlined in Tables 15 through 39 (Appendix H). The intent was to answer the two research questions that guided the current study. Chapter 5 will focus on the interpretation of the findings from the previous chapter and discuss the conclusion, limitations of the study, recommendations for future studies, and the significance of the findings to leadership.

Chapter 5

Conclusion and Recommendations

The purpose of this study was to explore the perceptions of a purposive sample of 10 Black Deaf male students and 10 alumni to decide if the SFP theory contributed to their pedagogic achievements. The subjects were students and alumni from a postsecondary institution in Washington, D.C. The main goal of this study was to explore the subjects' perceptions of their teachers' expectations, which was the foundation of the SFP theory influencing undergraduates or alumni academic pedagogy.

This chapter includes the research findings, interpretation of the data, implications of the findings, and recommendations. This chapter aligns the themes in Chapter 4 with Chapter 2's review of the literature. The significance of this study was to raise awareness about the achievement gap of the population of this study to educate advocates, policymakers, education leadership, and teachers. Prospective researchers, who are interested in the Black Deaf male academic experience as with similar research related to traditionally underrepresented groups with disabilities, could use this study as a benchmark.

Research Findings

Response rate. A qualitative survey was administered to 10 Black Deaf male undergraduates and 10 alumni. Each survey contained fifteen questions and fifteen commentary opportunities, which translated to 150 possible undergraduate participant comments and 150 possible alumni participant comments. Ninety two percent of alumni participants and 94% of undergraduate participants completed the survey. There were approximately 62% undergraduate comments and 88% alumni comments. The participant comments were analyzed using a six-step content analysis process in MS Excel and Word software. The following section presents the interpretation and implications of the findings.

Interpretation. The purpose of the survey questions was to understand the perceptions of Black Deaf males in the postsecondary setting. The interpretation was based on the qualitative descriptive analysis of the experience of the twenty participants who volunteered to complete the survey. The perceptions of the volunteers who completed the survey offered insights of their dyadic interactions with teachers in the classroom. The survey questions were intended to answer the two research questions related to the five SFP steps discussed in the review of the literature.

The participants of this study were Black Deaf male undergraduates and alumni. The populations of this study were American-born with a GPA between 2.0 and 4.0 (Oseguera, 2005). The undergraduates were current students at a higher education institution in Washington, D.C., and the alumni should have graduated from the same institution.

Implications. Creswell (2005) defined implications as "those suggestions for the importance of the study for different audiences" (p. 198). Cone and Foster (2006) added that implications were not necessarily intended to "prove or disprove a theory: They just support or fail to support it" (p. 275). In essence, Cone and Foster suggested that research implications offered the researcher an opportunity to present new ideas to existing theories and research.

A qualitative survey instrument was used to capture the perceptions of the population of the study. The research questions that guided this study were: (R1) how do

Black Deaf male students perceive a teacher's expectations of their academic performances in postsecondary institutions, and (R2) how do Black Deaf male students perceive teacher expectations influence achievements?

The specific problem was that the Black Deaf male student's perception of teacher expectations about his academic abilities and the teacher's expectations could be influencing his overall academic achievement. The population of this study had the lowest graduation rates among minorities (Gallaudet University Enrollment Reports 2000-2006; JBHE, 2007; U.S. Department of Education, 2009). The study participants responded to the survey questions and reflected on of their perceptions of teacher expectation influence on their pedagogy. The review of the literature, relevant background analysis, and the six-step content analysis process was used to analyze and code the data for emergent themes specific for this study.

Emergent Themes

The themes that emerged from the participants' survey were consistent with the five class, race, and achievement realities, the four-factor theory, and role models concepts and the five SFP steps discussed in the literature review (Ornstein & Levin, 1989; Tauber, 1997; Wooley & Bowen, 2007). The emergent themes were also consistent with the three educational theories. The data analysis identified 15 emergent themes: syllabic expectations, self-expectations, no-high-low expectations, eye-contact-acknowledgement, attitudinal indifference, public praise-positive-negative comments, personalized one-on-one attention, pop quiz reminders, office hours-after class counseling, team assignments, verbal-written-positive-negative feedback, private-public-verbal-written reinforcements, probing, reminders, and self-motivation. The participants of this study and comments to the survey along with the six-step content analysis process led to the development of these themes.

Theme 1: Syllabic expectations. The first emergent theme from the survey responses aligned with the first SFP step, which was the teacher formed an expectation, as discussed in the review of the literature (Tauber, 1997). The survey question asked the participants to identify how a teacher set expectations in the classroom. The classroom environment was aligned with the climate, as the environment was conducive to learning (Tauber, 1997). This theme also aligned with five class, race, and achievement realities in that a teacher might have formed expectations based on his or her mental model (Ornstein & Levine, 1989; Senge, 1990; Tauber, 1997).

The syllabic expectations theme meant that the teacher formed expectations in the classroom. Eleven (55%) participants indicated that the teacher formed expectations in the classroom with the course syllabus. This observation is congruent with the symbolic interactionist theory, which aimed to observe how student/teacher interact to identify causes that influence their academic performance or lack thereof.

In contrast to the interactionist theory were the functionalist and conflict educational theories. The three theories did not include ways expectations were formed. The functionalist theory posited that education was equitable and did not offer ways to form equitable education expectations. This was left up to the teachers. The conflict theory said that education was reserved for the elite and in-groups, and that was the expectation.

Theme 2: Self-expectations. The second theme also aligned with the first SFP step based on participant perception of positive examples that the teacher formed expectations. The survey question asked participants to give examples where the teacher formed expectations that *positively* influenced their classroom performance. Each participant's perception of how expectations were formed was consistent with the five class, race, and achievement realities, the four-factor theory, and mental model (Ornstein & Levine, 1989; Senge, 1990; Tauber, 1997).

The five class, race, and achievement realities posited that both teacher and student pre-conceived expectations based on the student's background influenced the educational outcomes. The outcomes were critical depending on the climate discussed in the four-factor theory. Therefore, participants' perceptions of whether the teacher used the syllabus to form expectation influenced their performance. Four (20%) participants perceived that the use of the syllabus *positively* influenced their performance.

The conflict theorist was built on the self-expectation theme in that the elites were expected to succeed because education was intended for them. The functionalist argued equitable education for all—self-expectation for all. The symbolic interactionist observed the classroom for self-expectation perceptions.

Theme 3: No/high/low expectations. The third theme identified from the participants, which aligned with the first SFP step, was intended to solicit negative examples the teacher used to form expectations. The survey question asked participants to give examples where the teacher formed expectations that *negatively* influenced their classroom performance. The literature review about the SFP painted an unenthusiastic picture that minorities were overrepresented in special education in addition to other challenges that this population faced.

Several examples were discussed related to the wide achievement gap of minorities in the review of the literature with respect to the five class, race, and achievement realities, the four-factor theory, and mental model (Ornstein & Levine, 1989; Senge, 1990; Tauber, 1997). The data analysis results were mixed. Five (25%) participants did not answer the question. Four (20%) participants noted that no expectations were set.

The no-high-low expectations themes were not in the conflict and functionalist theorist paradigms. The two theories focused on elitism and equitability that were often not afforded to minorities like the population of this study (see Chapter 2). The symbolic interactionist offered an engagement perspective through observations in the classroom to ensure that clear attainable expectations were formed.

The next section discusses themes associated with differential treatments within the five SFP steps. The first differential treatment was behavioral related and the second and third were Golem or Galatea effects. Differential treatments were cues such as body language and other props used to reinforce the formed expectations. The data analysis classified three themes for each differential treatment step.

Theme 4: Eye contact/acknowledgement. The fourth theme identified from the participants aligned with the second SFP step (Tauber, 1997). The survey question asked participants for the perception of their teachers' expectations of their academic performance. The intent of this question was to solicit communication cues. Communication cues were direct or indirect, supported the review of the literature.

The eye-contact acknowledgement theme was indirect communication. The communication needs of Deaf and hard of hearing required both direct use of ASL and indirect use of eye contact for effectiveness (McCaskill, 2005). Equally important was that poor communication, direct or indirect, affected identity development which was critical to achievement (Guyll et al., 2010).

According to Sarant et al. (2008), research has indicated that Deaf children learn language "only at 50%-60% of the rate of children with normal hearing and have at least one year language delay by the time they are school age" (p. 205). Language delay influences the Black Deaf male's ability to compete for resources, and educational and social opportunities, leads to poor academic performance in the classroom (Sarant et al., 2008; McCaskill, 2005). Communication was also viewed in a form of feedback within the four-factor theory.

The four-factor theory theorized that communication was affective or cognitive reinforcements, which was quality and quantity of reinforcements that was given to all students equally. The study identified 10 (50%) participants with the perception that teachers communicated high expectations. This was consistent with the functionalist education theory. The symbolic interactionist were observant of communication practices with respect to teachers that used communication to teach up to perceived bloomers and to teach down to perceived non-bloomers (Rosenthal & Jacobson, 1968). The conflict theorist contrasted the symbolic and functionalist theory with the notion that students were innately competitive beings that needed to compete with elites—otherwise, only elites were deserving of education (Beaver, 2009).

Theme 5: Attitudinal indifference. The fifth theme identified from the participants aligned with the second SFP step. The survey question asked the participants to provide examples of how the teacher communicated expectations of them with respect to non-verbal communication and attention. This theme aligned with the four-factor theory teacher's attention spread.

The notion was that the teacher provided equal teaching attention to all students regardless of all students' ability or disability (Tauber, 1997). Equal teacher attention is a non-verbal message, meant effective communication of expectations. Non-verbal communication was a necessity for the Deaf and Hard of Hearing student (McCaskill, 2005). Bailes et al. (2009) indicated that there are variations of ASL within the Deaf community similar to spoken accents that require adaptation—meaning that ineffective, indirect, unclear non-verbal communication could send the wrong message about expectations.

Ten (50%) participants of this study perceived that the teacher made eye contact that showed that she or he cared about their learning. This theme was clear to the conflict theorist expectation in that the non-verbal message was that one had to be elite to reap the benefits of education. None of the elites were excluded. The functional theorist non-verbal message was equal education access for all. In practice, the functionalist failed to take noticed that minorities were overrepresented in special education programs. The symbolic interactionist non-verbal message was to observe dyadic interaction between teacher and student to identify the effectiveness of non-verbal communication.

Theme 6: Public praise - positive/negative comments. The sixth theme identified from this study supported the second SFP step. The survey question asked participants to describe an example that indicated that the teacher cared about their learning in the classroom. This theme was congruent with the output discussed in the four-factor theory (Tauber, 1997). The theory, related to verbal and non-verbal communication, posited that teachers used prompts, probes, and opportune all students to learn (Tauber, 1997).

The teacher's ability to opportune all students to learn were congruent with the good intentions of the NCLB, IDEA, and ADA (Darling-Hammond, 2004; Hunter & Bartee, 2003; Matthews, 2005). Researchers have argued that there were educational disparities and achievement gap concerned in education policies (Darling-Hammond, 2004; Hunter & Bartee, 2003; Matthews, 2005). The educational disparities spoke to the notion that some teachers did not opportune all students to learn once the expectations were formed.

Eleven (55%) of the participants perceived that teachers used various prompts to support the formed expectations. The prompts included simple acknowledgements, inquiries, and office hour opportunities. The functionalist viewed outputs to validate its position about equal education. The conflict theorist perspective contrasted the functionalist in that elites did not need the teacher's verbal and no-verbal cues. Elites were thought to be smart because they had access to quality education, which was reserved for them. The symbolic interactionist studied the teacher's verbal and non-verbal cues to ensure that all students received "fair" teacher outputs.

The next SFP step was differential treatment that the teacher used to communicate to the student what behaviors and achievements were expected. The study analysis resulted in three themes. The themes were personalized one-on-one attention, pop quiz reminders, and office hours-after class counseling.

Theme 7: Personalized one-on-one attention. The seventh theme identified from the participants aligned with the third SFP step (Tauber, 1997). The question from this study asked the participants to provide an example of how the teacher's feedback discouraged them and led them to fail. This theme was parallel to the review of the literature.

The literature related to minority education and achievement gap was clear in stating that minorities were overrepresented in special education. The overrepresentation meant more focus on education and its quality was given to Whites and elites and less educational attention to minorities. The overrepresentation contrasted the four-factor theory perspective. This perspective was that teachers gave affective and cognitive reinforcement, attention, and verbal and non-verbal cues to all students to aid their academic success (Tauber, 1997).

This was not true from the historical perspective discussed in the literature. Minorities were nonexistent in education until recently due to biased practices and neglect (Buhanan, 1999). Six (30%) of the participants stated that teachers did not give them feedback after grading their assignments. Feedback, affective and cognitive was critical to the student's self-perception of success and learning (Tauber, 1997).

The conflict theorist sent a non-verbal feedback to the world that only elites were worthy of education. This view proposed the notion that elitist did not need one-on-one attention because they were smart. The functionalists advocated and sided with the four-factor theory feedback, input, and output for all (Tauber, 1997). The symbolic interactionist and the SFP researchers highlighted disparities with close observation of the teacher and student interaction (Hinnant et al., 2009; Jussim & Harber, 2005; Merton, 1948; Rosenthal & Jacobson, 1968; Smit & Fritz, 2008; Tauber, 1997).

Themes 8 and 9: Pop quiz reminders and office hours/after class counseling.
The eighth and ninth themes that this study analysis identified supported the third SFP step. The question asked the participants to identify how their teacher responded when they did not perform as expected. The results were congruent with several perspectives that were reviewed in Chapter 2 with respect to the Golem effects.

Tauber (1997) discussed the importance of this theme in terms of opportunities where the teacher could have unintentionally used this theme to help perceived achievers. Rosenthal and Jacobson (1968) added that this theme could have been the culprit to the result from their bloomers and non-bloomers experiment. The notion was that teachers used this theme to help perceived bloomers by providing affective and cognitive reinforcements, more attention, and verbal and non-verbal cues (Rosenthal & Jacobson, 1968; Tauber, 1997).

Six (30%) of the participants perceived that teachers gave them positive verbal and disappointed remarks and helped them after class. Five (25%) of the participants perceived that teachers wrote disappointing remarks on their homework and helped them after class. Four (20%) of the participants perceived that teachers were disappointed and did not follow up. These mixed findings were congruent with the Golem and Galatea effects arguments in the literature.

The symbolic interactionist was interested in finding out why different students had different perceptions during dyadic interactions. The functionalist was not concerned about the different perceptions as long as all of the students received equal education. The conflict theorist would have affirmed its position that elites, who were considered smarter than non-elites, would have aced their quizzes and did not need reminders to succeed.

The next SFP step was if treatment was consistent over time, and if the student did not actively resist, it tended to shape his or her behavior or achievement. The study analysis resulted in three themes: team assignments, verbal-written-positive-negative feedback, and private-public-verbal-written reinforcements.

Theme 10: Team assignments. The tenth theme that the participants identified was parallel to the fourth SFP step. The question asked the participants to indicate class activities the teacher used to help them succeed in class. The findings aligned with the Galatea effects perspective in the literature.

This theme made reference to bloomers and non-bloomers and the five class, race, and achievement realities (Ornstein & Levine, 1989; Rosenthal & Jacobson, 1968). According to the bloomers and non-bloomers, the teachers were told *a priori* that a group of students were bloomers to test the SFP theory in an experiment. At the end of the experiment, the teachers reported that bloomers were happy and upbeat (Rosenthal & Jacobson, 1968).

The five class, race, and achievement realities alluded that teachers could have used ineffective instructional groupings (Ornstein & Levin, 1989). 10 (50%) of the student participants countered the ineffective instructional groupings and bloomers perspective. The participants perceived that teachers assigned them to teams and followed up with them to ensure their participation. The three educational theories were congruent with the participants' perceptions in that the findings were positive.

Theme 11: Verbal/written – positive/negative feedback. The eleventh theme identified from participants was fitted with the fourth SFP step. Two survey questions were asked. The first survey question asked participants to identify how the teacher's feedback encouraged them to succeed in the classroom. The second survey question asked the participants how the teacher encouraged them to perform better than their classmates. The review of the literature compared and contrasted the Golem and Galatea effects related to this theme.

The Galatea-effect literature argued positive teacher expectations, and other variables such as verbal praise and other external rewards, should have been considered (Rubie-Davies et al., 2006). Galatea-effect supporters speculated that formative feedback was *a posteriori*, improved the student's learning experience (Rubie-Davies et al., 2006). The formative feedback argument was similar to the four-factor theory feedback, input, and output (Rubie-Davies et al., 2006; Tauber, 1997).

The findings from the first question were that 10 (50%) of the participants perceived that the teacher gave verbal and written feedback on assignments. This was congruent with the quality and quantity reinforcement and the symbolic interactionist observation. Three (15%) participants perceived that feedback was consistent, which is on point with the SFP step 4. Three (15%) perceived that feedback was given in public. The functionalist and conflict theorist omitted feedback as part of their paradigm. The two theories focused on equal education and elitist and failed to discuss how it was practiced.

The findings from the second question indicated that six (30%) of the participants perceived that teachers publicly gave them feedback. The public feedback perception referred to the review of the literature discussion about role models and self-esteem building. This aligned with the symbolic interactionist theory in terms of affective and cognitive reinforcements (Tauber, 1997). Seven (35%) of the participants had the perception that teachers offered generic feedback to all. The generic feedback perceptions supported the functionalist theory similar to proving equal teaching attention to all students regardless of ability or disability (Tauber, 1997). Three (15%) of the participants had the perception that they cared about their education and did not depend on the teacher's expectation and differential treatment. The conflict theorist would have enjoyed these participants that sounded like elitists.

Theme 12: Private/public - verbal/written reinforcements. The twelfth theme identified by the participants was fitting to the fourth SFP step. The question asked the participants how the teacher responded to them when they performed above expectations. The review of the literature discussed the Galatea effects and the cultural dualism perspectives.

The discussion focused on the climate and culture of school and cautioned that there was more to the disparities that went beyond the Golem effects argument. The goal was to offer a holistic perspective to some of the factors that impact minorities in academia. Nieto (2009) indicated that a school climate was a learning environment with clear expectations of what behaviors were accepted, or unaccepted, and rewarded, or unrewarded.

These were reinforcements depending on the climate that was identified in the four-factor theory (Tauber, 1997). Nine (45%) of the participants perceived that positive reinforcements were offered in private and seven (35%) perceived that positive comments were written on their papers. The functionalist viewed reinforcements in terms of rewards, while conflict theorists contrasted this point of view with the need for quality education. The symbolic interactionalist viewed feedback as a positive outcome of the dyadic interaction between the teacher and student.

The final SFP step was that with time, the student's behavior and achievement would conform closer to what was expected of him or her. The study analysis resulted in three themes: probing, reminders, and self-motivation.

Theme 13: Probing. The thirteenth theme identified by the participants aligned with the fifth SFP step. The questions asked participants to identify class activities that the teacher used to help them feel academically challenged. The review of the literature identified the four-factor theory.

The four-factor theory discussed the output in which the teacher used prompts, probes, and opportune all students to learn. The literature discussed various opportunities where authority figures and role models used probing to enhance achievement. Five (25%) of the participants perceived that they were called on to answer and were probed. This is parallel to the symbolic interactionist observation of positive dyadic interaction. The functionalist viewed probing as a necessity to earn a reward. The conflict theorist did not discuss probing; rather, it focused on finding quality education for elites.

Theme 14: Reminders. The fourteenth theme identified from the participants was related to the fifth SFP step. The question asked participants to describe an example that showed that they succeeded academically because of the teacher's expectations. This theme was discussed in the literature.

The literature was explicit with the discussion about how teachers who practiced Golem- effect SFP used reminders to ensure negative SFP prophecies were fulfilled. Some examples included overrepresentation in special education, generic labeling, disparities in teaching approaches, and educational policies that caused the achievement gap to widen – prophecy fulfilled. Four (20%) of the participants perceived that teachers reminded them about expectations. Seven (35%) of the participants perceived that teachers gave them one-on-one attention to remind them about expectations.

The conflict theorist focused on quality education was not concerned with this theme. This was a reminder to the world that only elites were expected to gain access to education. This expectation was clear from the start. The functionalist theorist was concerned about equal education for all. The reminder was that all were entitled to education. The symbolic interactionist was concerned with observing the classroom interaction between the teacher and the student to ensure that learning took place. The reminder was to consider all factors that could contribute to achievement or lack thereof. The basic premise of this theme was to ensure that the SFP step one was fulfilled.

Theme 15: Self-motivation. The final theme from the analysis of this study was intended to solicit participants' perception about Golem effects. The question asked participants to provide an example that showed that they failed academically because of the teacher's expectation. The literature discussion was comprehensive about Golem-effect impact on minorities (see Chapter 2).

Most of the review of the literature focused on the Golem effects perspective and provided research discussions about the widening achievement gap of minorities compared to their peers. Tauber (1997) conceptualized the five SFP steps and noted in step 4 that if the student did not actively resist, it tended to shape his or her behavior and then in step 5, the student's behavior and achievement conformed more closely to what was expected of him. Brown (2006), Buller (2007), Popp (2005), and Wong and Hui (2006) stated that Merton originally conceptualized the SFP as a contributor to social problems. The social problems included racial prejudice, discrimination in education and the workplace, and economic recessions.

The population of this study had the lowest graduation rates of any group among approximately 13.2% of Black males with disabilities that enrolled in postsecondary education during a 6-year time frame (Gallaudet University Enrollment Reports 2000-2006; JBHE, 2007; U.S. Department of Education, 2007). The Golem effects literature stereotyped this study population under false assumptions that they have similar needs as Black hearing males (Harper & Nichols, 2008).

To that end, the final theme sought to identify if the Golem effects impacted the population of this study. The results from the participants addressing this theme were not significant to support Golem effects. Four (20%) of the participants perceived that their teacher shared discouraging words. Five (25%) of the participants did not answer the question. The participants' perception of the last question along with perceptions throughout this study led to the implication of this theme.

Limitations

According to Creswell (2005), limitations are problems and weaknesses that the researcher identified during the course of the research. The first limitation was that the research participants volunteered to participate. The second was that some of the participants did not expand on their perceptions in addition to survey choices. The third was that the participants had various K-12 education foundations that could have impacted the results with respect to articulation of the meaning of the SFP. The final limitation was that the research focused on American-born Black Deaf males, limiting results to the United States.

Recommendations

This study was expected to generate awareness among education advocates, policymakers, educational leadership, and teachers about the impact of the SFP theory on the academic achievement of Black Deaf male students in higher education. The outcomes were intended to direct attention on how improvement can be made to statistical reporting systems and faculty development training programs, and to develop new policies to heighten minority student retention in postsecondary institutions. The research results of this research anticipated outlining coping strategies for Black Deaf male students in postsecondary environments.

Details of the perception of a purposive sample of 10 undergraduate and 10 alumni Black Deaf male students in higher education settings were presented. The minutiae offered Galatea effects techniques that the subjects are using or were used to achieve their pedagogic goals. These elements should serve as standards to other Black Deaf males in higher education.

Recommendations for Black Deaf male students. Respondents in this study offered several coping strategies for traversing higher education settings that had positive SFP or Galatea effects. These strategies might or might not have been effectual for every Black Deaf male; however, these strategies offer an opportunity for the population of this study and traditionally underrepresented groups a place to start. Most of the participants in this analysis had the perception that active participation on their parts in the academic experience was critical to success or failure. Most participants also agreed that being dependent on teacher expectations alone was not a good idea.

It is recommended that a Black Deaf male student in higher education find a mentor or a role model, be it a faculty, staff, a graduate student, or a peer. The intent would be to help them recognize that they can resist the Golem-effect SFP as freshmen. The mentor or role model could also help them appreciate or recognize their freshman status as a symbol of academic achievement, and that persistence is the key to graduation.

Recommendations for faculty. University faculty members were not the focus of this study. However, they were perceived as role models for students. The participants in this analysis commented that their instructors made a difference in their academic experiences. Most of the participants felt cared for and challenged, and appreciated the faculty who took interest in them. Most of the participants in this inquiry perceived that faculty used Galatea-effect SFP principles to help them succeed.

It is recommended that faculty became more aware of how Black Deaf male students perceive them based on these research findings. They should continue challenging all students, especially traditionally underrepresented students. Faculty members are encouraged to share success stories and tip to enhance this group's success at faculty development training events. Sharing success stories are ways to minimize and influence other faculty who may carry hidden, implicit stereotypes. Faculty members should also consider using the findings to begin mentoring and serving as role models to the population of this study and other traditionally underrepresented students.

Recommendations for higher education leaders. The research and survey questions and emerging themes were intended to prompt educate advocates, policymakers, educational leadership, and teachers about the impact of the SFP theory on the academic achievement of Black Deaf male students in higher education. The foremost nature of this study was to serve as a strategic development foundation. Higher education leaders should use the findings to improve statistical reporting systems.

These systems can focus on analyzing specific traditionally underrepresented groups' pedagogic experience. The intent can be to avoid generic categorizations of minorities such as Deaf and hard of hearing people, special education students, intellectual disorders, and other disabilities (U.S. Department of Education, 2007, 2010). Each of these categories had different academic needs (Harper and Nichols, 2008).

It is recommended that higher education leaders commission further research on why Black Deaf male students' achievements are among the lowest of their cohorts or comparable groups (Gallaudet University Annual Enrollment Reports, 2000-2006; JBHE, 2007; U.S. Department of Education, 2007). Hearing loss does not define ability. Black Deaf males have capabilities that are largely unexplored because the majority is overrepresented in special education programs as a result of assumptions about hearing loss, which overshadows their capabilities (Sears, 2008; U.S. Department of Education, 2007, 2010).

Another recommendation is for higher education leaders to examine existing statistical reporting systems that apply generic labels to traditionally underrepresented groups. These types of reporting systems camouflage critical underlying issues about this group. The generic labels and reporting systems often lead to erroneous assumptions about this group, assumptions that are often gone unnoticed until too late. Harper and Nichols (2008) stated, "An enormous assumption is often made that Black men, one of the most stereotyped groups on college and university campuses, all share common experiences and backgrounds" (p. 199).

A final recommendation for leadership and leaders in higher education is to dramatically increase Black Deaf males in the leadership ranks. This bold move requires that administrators look beyond the stereotype that Black males belong in prisons (Maxwell, 2012). Along with other stereotypes typically relate to Black men, this view serves only to reinforce the SFP phenomenon. Maxwell added, "Another significant factor was a transition to college that included high expectations from administrators and faculty and from successful black male juniors and seniors on campus who motivated them" (p. 1). Some of these administrators could be Black men who could have served as role models to entering Black male freshmen.

Recommendations for future research. This study focused on a purposive sample of 10 undergraduates and 10 alumni Black Deaf male students in a higher education institution in Washington, D. C. The first recommendation is that future researchers consider increasing the sample size and scope of this investigation. The next recommendation is that future studies include a combination of a survey and an interview to follow up on the participants. Following up would have helped verify some of the survey responses.

A third recommendation is to survey faculty to learn of their perceptions of how they cope(d) with traditionally underrepresented groups, especially those who have not had such students in their classrooms. The fourth recommendation is to use this study as a benchmark to conduct SFP research focusing on other traditionally underrepresented groups with disabilities such as Latino and Asian populations. Finally, if this study is replicated, it is recommended that demographics such as academic term and cumulative GPA data be included.

Significance to Leadership

Implementation of the findings from this research may offer several potential benefits to higher education leadership. The first benefit is financial-related. Numerous researchers discussed the impact of costs of enrolling in higher education with respect to cost to students and loan repayments, cost to the institution, its impact on enrollment, and research (Beath, Poyago-Theotoky, & Ulph, 2012; Martin, 2012). These researchers posited the cost benefits stemmed from the wealth of knowledge that higher education added to society. Higher education leadership analysis of cost per student could have been considerate of the high numbers of minority dropouts (Hrabowski III et al., 1998).

The second benefit is related to the notion that graduates from higher education are trained and expected to be productive members of society (Beath, Poyago-Theotoky, & Ulph, 2012). Higher education knowledge and skills was a navigational compass to social advancement and status (Breen, 2010). Drucker (1999) added, "The most valuable asset of a 21st century institution (whether business or non-business) will be its *knowledge workers* and their *productivity*" (p. 79). Rowley, Lujan, and Dolence (1997) stated, "Learning will be the primary means by which individuals succeed in society. Those who learn will flourish. Those who do not will possibly sink" (p. 13).

The final benefit is humane-related in that developing programs for the Black Deaf student to improve his pedagogic achievement is the right thing to do. With the proliferation of the Internet, society became interconnected on many levels. This interconnectedness revealed opportunities to combine our abilities as humans. Rather than overrepresentation in special education, higher education leadership should do the right thing and use the emergent themes to design programs to help traditionally underrepresented groups to become productive members of society—a promise often expressed in most higher education institution missions.

Conclusion

This qualitative descriptive study attained its research objectives. The intent was to explore the perceptions of a purposive sample of Black Deaf male students in a postsecondary setting in Washington, D.C. to determine if the SFP theory contributed to their pedagogic achievements. Administering and collecting the survey, coding the responses into SFP themes, and using a six-step content analysis method steered to the achievement of the research objectives.

The two research questions that guided this exploration and emergent themes were: (R1) how do Black Deaf male students perceive a teacher's expectations of their academic performances in postsecondary institutions, and (R2) how do Black Deaf male students perceive teacher expectations influence on their achievements? The first question investigated perceived SFP themes as factors that influenced the Black Deaf male student's academic performance in a postsecondary setting.

The three themes that emerged from this question were syllabic expectations, self-expectations, and no-high-low expectations. These themes associated with the Tauber (1997) SFP step 1 and how a teacher forms expectations. Three matching survey questions guided R1 (Table 15, Appendix H).

The second question explored perceived teacher expectations that influenced their academic achievements. Twelve themes emerged from R2. The twelve themes were analyzed based on the remaining four SFP steps. The three themes that emerged from SFP step two related to R2 were eye contact-acknowledgement, attitudinal indifference, and public praise-positive-negative comments. Three analogous survey questions can be found in Table 16, Appendix H.

SFP step three themes related to R2 were personalized one-on-one attention, pop quiz reminders, and office hours-after class counseling. The two equivalent survey questions can be found in Table 17, Appendix H. SFP step four themes connected to R2 were team assignments, verbal-written-positive-negative feedback, and private-public-verbal-written reinforcements. The four corresponding survey questions can be found in Table 18, Appendix H. The final SFP step five themes were probing, reminders, and self-motivation. The three related survey questions can be found in Table 19, Appendix H.

The outcomes highlighted coping strategies in postsecondary setting for Black Deaf male students. The point was that education was a collaborative effort between teacher and student, which was evident in the responses and comments. These strategies should have served as a standard for other Black Deaf male K-12 students. Future research on this population should have expanded the sample size and scope, include demographic information such as term and cumulative GPA, and added a follow-up interview to the survey questions.

Finally, the research findings were parallel to Galatea-effect SFP literature even though numerous researches had focused on the Golem-effect SFP (Al-Fadhi & Singh,

2006; Couch, 2010; Jussim & Harber, 2005; Riley & Ungerleider, 2008; Rubie-Davies et al., 2006; Rubie-Davies, Peterson, Irving, Widdowson, & Dixon, 2010; Tsiplakides & Keramida, 2010; Willard, Madon, Guyll, Spoth, & Jussim, 2008; Wong & Hui, 2006). Galatea effects were positive expectations that were reinforced with positive differential treatment such as the emergent themes (Rubie-Davies et al.; Table 9; p. 74). The participants in this study responded and commented that their educational experience were positive, which was congruent to Galatea effects SFP.

References

Aksan, N., Kisac, B., Aydin, M., & Demirbuken, S. (2009). Symbolic interaction theory. *Procedia Social and Behavioral Science, 1*(1), 902-904. doi: 10.1016/j.sbspro.2009.01.160

Al-Fadhli, H., & Singh, M. (2006). Teachers' expectancy and efficacy as correlates of school achievement in Delta, Mississippi. *Journal of Personnel Evaluation in Education, 19*(1-2), 51-67. Retrieved from http://ejournals.ebsco.com/direct.asp?ArticleID=41FC9206BE03E473D38F

Amouroux, R. (2010). Marie Bonaparte, her first two patients and the literary world. *The International Journal of Psychoanalysis, 91*(4), 879-894. doi: 10.1111/j.1745-8315.2010.00278.x

Anderson, C. B., & Smart, J. F. (2010). Improving transition outcomes for culturally and linguistically diverse VR consumers. *Journal of Applied Rehabilitation Counseling, 41*(4), 3-10. Retrieved from http://search.proquest.com/docview/846726225?accountid=35812

Anderson, G. B., & Miller, K. R. (2004). In their own words: Researching stories about the lives of Deaf people of color. *Multicultural Perspectives, 6*(2), 28-33. doi: abs/10.1207/s15327892mcp0602_6

Arum, R., Beattie, I., & Ford, K. (2011). *The structure of schooling.* (2nd ed). Thousand Oaks, CA: Sage.

Baglieri, S., & Moses, A. (2010). "My name is Jay": On teachers' roles in the overrepresentation of minorities in special education and what teacher education can do. *Disability Studies Quarterly, 30*(2), 15-22. Retrieved from http://dsq-sds.org/article/view/1243/1287

Bailes, C. N., Erting, C. J., Erting, L. C., & Thumann-Prezioso, C. (2009). Language and literacy acquisition through parental mediation in American Sign Language. *Sign Language Studies, 9*(4), 417-456. doi:10.1353/sls.0.0022

Balfanz, R., Legters, N., West, T. C., & Weber, L. M. (2007). Are NCLS' measures, incentives, and improvement strategies the right ones for the nation's low-performing high schools? *American Educational Research Journal, 44*(3), 559-593. Retrieved from http://search.proquest.com/docview/200369397?accountid=35812

Baxley, T. P. (2008). "What are you?" Biracial children in the classroom. *Childhood Education, 84*(4), 230-233. Retrieved from http://search.proquest.com/docview/210393327?accountid=35812

Beath, J. A., Poyago-Theotoky, J., and Ulph, D. (2012) University funding systems: Impact on research and teaching. *Economics: The Open-Access, Open-Assessment E-Journal, 6*(2). doi: http://dx.doi.org/10.5018/economics-ejournal.ja.2012-2

Beaver, W. (2009). For-profit higher education: A social and historical analysis. *Sociological Viewpoint, 25,* 53-73. Retrieved from http://search.proquest.com/docview/221242597?accountid=35812

Becker, D. (2010). The impact of teachers' expectations on students' educational opportunities in the life course: An empirical test of a subjective-expected-utility explanation (Working paper). *Management, Economics and Social Science, 1*(7), 1-43. Retrieved from http://www.cgs.uni-koeln.de/fileadmin/wiso_fak/cgs/pdf/working_paper/cgswp_01-07.pdf

Bembenutty, H. (2008). The last word: The scholar whose expectancy-value theory transformed the understanding of adolescence, gender differences, and achievement: An interview with Jacquelynne S. Eccles. *Journal of Advance Academics, 19*(3), 531-550. Retrieved from http://search.proquest.com/docview/222696391?accountid=35812

Breen, R. (2010). Educational expansion and social mobility in the 20th century. *Social Forces, 89*(2), 365-388. Retrieved from http://search.proquest.com/docview/859591960?accountid=35812

Brown, D. A. (2006). *The role of pop culture-based information and stereotypes versus direct knowledge of individuals in forming teacher expectations of African American students* The University of North Carolina at Greensboro. *ProQuest Dissertations and Theses,* 218 p. Retrieved from http://search.proquest.com/docview/305284578?accountid=35812

Brown, G. F., Mangelsdorf, S. C., Neff, C., Schoppe-Sullivan, S. J., & Frosch, C. A. (2009). Young children's self-concepts: Associations with child temperament, mothers' and fathers' parenting, and triadic family interaction. *Merrill-Palmer Quarterly, 55*(2), 182-216. doi: 10.1353/mpq.0.0019

Buchanan, R. M. (1999). *Illusions of equality: Deaf Americans in school and factory. 1850-1950.* Washington, DC: Gallaudet University Press.

Buller, A. A. (2007). *Expectancy confirmation effects: Accumulation and moderation by social interaction.* Iowa State University. *ProQuest Dissertations and Theses,* Retrieved from http://search.proquest.com/docview/304859093?accountid=35812

Campbell, S., & Roden, J. (2010). Research approaches for novice nephrology nurse researchers. *Renal Society of Australasia Journal, 6*(3), 114-120. Retrieved from http://www.renalsociety.org/RSAJ/journal/nov10/campbell.pdf

Castellan, C. M. (2010). Quantitative and qualitative research: A view for clarity. *International Journal of Education, 2*(2), 1-14. Retrieved from http://www.macrothink.org/journal/index.php/ije/article/viewFile/446/361

Caufield, J. (2007). What motivates students to provide feedback to teachers about teaching and learning? An expectancy theory perspective. *International Journal for the Scholarship of Teaching and Learning. 1*(1), 1-19. Retrieved from http://academics.georgiasouthern.edu/ijsotl/v1n1/caulfield/IJ_Caulfield.pdf

Compton-Lilly, C. (2011). Literacy and schooling in one family across time. *Research in theTeaching of English, 45*(3), 224-251. Retrieved from http://search.proquest.com/docview/849266511?accountid=35812

Cone, J. D., & Foster, S. L. (2006). *Dissertation from start to finish: Psychology and related fields.* (2nd ed.) Washington, DC: American Psychology Association

Cooper, D., & Schindler, P. (2003). *Business research methods* (8th ed.). Boston, MA: McGraw Hill/Irwin.

Cosby, B., & Poussaint, A. F. (2007). *Come on people.* Nashville, TN: Thomas Nelson, Inc.

Couch, M. (2010). *First grade teachers' perceptions of and expectations for ELL students*. Walden University. *ProQuest Dissertations and Theses*. Retrieved from http://search.proquest.com/docview/305224931?accountid=35812

Creswell, J. W. (2005). *Educational research: Planning, conducting, and evaluating quantitative and qualitative research* (2nd ed.). Upper Saddle River, NJ: Prentice Hall.

Creswell, J. W. (2009). *Research design: Qualitative, quantitative, and mixed methods approaches*. (3rd ed.). Thousand Oaks, CA: Sage.

Crossley, N. (2010). Networks and complexity: Directions for interactionist research? *Symbolic Interaction, 33*(3), 341-363. doi: 10.1525/si.2010.33.3.341.342

Darling-Hammond, L. (2004). The color line in American education: The color line in American education. *Du Bois Review, 1*(2), 213-246. Retrieved from http://search.proquest.com/docview/214850898?accountid=35812

De' Armond, D. (2011). An empirical examination of preference for numerical information and need for emotion within financial planning. *The Journal of American Academy of Business, 16*(2), 287-295. Retrieved from http://search.proquest.com/docview/817185202?accountid=35812

de Boer, H., Bosker, R. J., & van der Werf, M. P. C. (2010). Sustainability of teacher expectation bias effects on long-term student performance. *Journal of Educational Psychology, 102*(1), 168-179. doi: 10.1037/a0017289

DeCuir-Gunby, J. T. (2009). A review of the racial identity development of African American adolescents: The role of education. *Review of Educational Research, 79*(1), 103-124. doi: 10.3102/0034654308325897

Drucker, P. F. (1999). Knowledge-worker productivity: The biggest challenge. *California Management Review, 41*(2), 79-93. Retrieved from http://search.proquest.com/docview/216137821?accountid=35812

Eiser, J. R., Stafford, T., & Fazio, R. H. (2008). Expectancy confirmation in attitude learning: A connectionist account. *European Journal of Social Psychology, 38,* 1023-1032. doi: 10.1002/ejsp.530

Erickson, E. H. (1968). *Identity youth and crisis.* New York, NY: W. W. Norton.

Eyler, L. T., & Jeste, D. V. (2006). Enhancing the informed consent process: A conceptual overview. *Behavioral Science and Law, 24,* 553-568. doi: 10.1002/bsl.691

Faber, N. K. (2006). Conducting qualitative research: A practical guide for school counselors. *Professional School Counseling, 9*(5), 367-375. Retrieved from http://search.proquest.com/docview/213312125?accountid=35812

Ferri, B. A., & Connor, D. J. (2005). In the shadow of Brown: Special education and overrepresentation of students of color. *Remedial and Special Education, 26*(2), 93-100. Retrieved from http://search.proquest.com/docview/236331928?accountid=35812

Fortune, L. D., & Gillespie, E. (2010). The influence of practice standards on massage therapists' work experience: A descriptive pilot study. *International Journal of Therapeutic Massage & Bodywork: Research, Education, & Practice, 3*(3), 1-11. Retrieved from http://www.ijtmb.org/index.php/ijtmb/article/view/73/120

Gallaudet University Annual Enrollment Reports. (2009). Retrieved from http://www.gallaudet.edu/Office_of_Academic_Quality/Institutional_Research/Annual_Enrollment_Reports.html

Gallaudet University Annual Enrollment Reports. (2008).

http://www.gallaudet.edu/Office_of_Academic_Quality/Institutional_Research/Annual_Enrollment_Reports.html

Gallaudet University Annual Enrollment Reports. (2000-2006). Retrieved from http://www.gallaudet.edu/Office_of_Academic_Quality/Institutional_Research/Annual_Enrollment_Reports.html

Germain, L., & Quinn, D. (2005). Investigation of tacit knowledge in principal leadership. *The Educational Forum, 70*(1), 75-91. doi: 10.1080/00131720508984873

Goar, H. (2009). *The Thomas Theorem*. Retrieved from http://search.ebscohost.com

Green, T. D. (2005). Promising prevention and early intervention strategies to reduce overrepresentation of African American students in special education. *Preventing School Failure, 49*(3), 33-41. Retrieved from http://search.proquest.com/docview/228518976?accountid=35812

Gubrium, J. F., & Holstein, J. A. (1997). *The active interview*. Thousand Oaks, CA: Sage

Guyll, M., Madon, S., Prieto, L., & Scherr, K. C. (2010). The potential roles of self-fulfilling prophecies, stigma consciousness, and stereotype threat in linking Latino/a ethnicity and educational outcomes. *Journal of Social Issues, 66*(1), 113-130. doi: 10.1111/j.1540-4560.2009.01636.x

Harper, S., & Nichols, A. (2008). Are they not all the same? Racial heterogeneity among black male undergraduates. *Journal of College Student Development, 49*(3), 199-

214. Retrieved from

http://repository.upenn.edu/cgi/viewcontent.cgi?article=1156&context=gse_pubs

Harris, C. K. (2005). The impact of zero tolerance and racial profiling as it relates to United States public education of African American students in elementary and secondary schools. *Proceedings of the Academy of Educational Leadership, 10*(2), 55-58. Retrieved from

http://www.sbaer.uca.edu/research/allied/2005vegas/edu%20ldrship/12.pdf

Hawes, R. J. (2005). *The self-fulfilling prophecy in college athletics.* Retrieved from http://www.smcm.edu/psyc/_assets/documents/SMP/Showcase/0405-RHawes.pdf

Hershovitz, S. (2010). Harry Potter and the trouble with tort theory. *Stanford Law Review*, Forthcoming; University of Michigan Public Law Working Paper No. 219; University of Michigan Law & Economics, Empirical Legal Studies Center Paper No. 10-027. Retrieved from http://ssrn.com/abstract=1687923

Hinnant, J. B., O'Brien, M., & Ghazarian, S. R. (2009). The longitudinal relations of teacher expectations to achievement in the early school years. *Journal of Educational Psychology, 101*(3), 662-670. Retrieved from http://www.ncbi.nlm.nih.gov/pmc/articles/PMC2860190/

Hjelmeland, H., & Knizek, B. L. (2010). Why we need qualitative research in suicidology. *Suicide and Life-Threatening Behavior, 40*(1), 74-80. Retrieved from http://search.proquest.com/docview/224886892?accountid=35812

Hout, M. (2011). Social and economic returns to college education. *Annual Review of Sociology, 37*, 1-45. doi: 10.1146/annurev.soc.012809.102503

Hoy, W. K. (2009). *Quantitative research in education: A primer*. Thousand Oaks, CA: SAGE.

Hrabowski, III, F. A., Maton, K. I., & Greif, G. L. (1998). *Beating the odds: Raising academically successful African American males*. New York, NY: Oxford University Press.

Hsieh, H. F., & Shannon, S. E. (2005). Three approaches to qualitative content analysis. *Qualitative Health Research, 15*(9), 1277-1288. Doi: 10.1177/104932305276687

Hunter, R. C., & Bartee, R. (2003). The achievement gap: Issues of competition, class, and race. *Education and Urban Society, 35*(2), 151-160. doi: 10.1177/0013124502239389

Jackson, R. L., II, Drummond, D. K., & Camara, S. (2007). What is qualitative research? *Qualitative Research Reports in Communication, 8*(1), 21-28. Doi:10.1080/1745930701617879

Jambor, E., & Elliott, M. (2005). Self-esteem and coping strategies among deaf students. *Journal of Deaf Studies and Deaf Education, 10*(1), 63-81. doi: 10.1093/deafed/eni004

James, A. R., Kellman, M., & Lieberman, L. (2011). Perspectives on inclusion from students with disabilities and responsive strategies for teachers. *Journal of Physical Education, Recreation, & Dance, 82*(1), 33-38. Retrieved from http://go.galegroup.com/ps/i.do?id=GALE%7CA247635311&v=2.1&u=wash751 04&it=r&p=PROF&sw=w

JBHE. (2007). Black student college graduation rates inch higher but a large racial gap persists. *The Journal of Blacks in Higher Education Online.* Retrieved from http://www.jbhe.com/preview/winter07preview.html

Johnson, J. R., & McIntosh, A. S. (2009). Toward a cultural perspective and understanding of the disability and deaf experience in special and multicultural education. *Remedial and Special Education, 30*(2). doi: 10.1177/0741932508324405

Josselson, R. (1987). *Finding herself: Pathways to identity development in women. The Jossey-Bass social and behavioral science series.* San Francisco, CA: Jossey-Bass.

Jowers, S. (2005). *Ending the educational exile of black deaf children from Washington, D.C.: Miller v. Board of Education of the District of Columbia.* Howard University). *ProQuest Dissertations and Theses,* 330. Retrieved from http://search.proquest.com/docview/305000992?accountid=35812

Jussim, L., & Harber, K. D. (2005). Teacher expectations and self-fulfilling prophecies: Knowns and unknowns, resolved and unresolved controversies. *Personality and Social Psychology Review, 9*(2), 131-155. doi: 10.1207/s15327957pspr0902_3

Karami, A., Rowley, J., & Analoui, F. (2006). Research and knowledge building in management studies: An analysis of methodological preferences. *International Journal of Management, 23*(1), 43- 52. Retrieved from http://search.proquest.com/docview/233230661?accountid=27346

Kautsky, J. H. (1965). Myth, self-fulfilling prophecy, and symbolic reassurance in the East-West conflict. *The Journal of Conflict Resolution (pre-1986), 9*(1), 1. doi: 10.1177/002200276500900101

Khoo, O. (2010). Diaspora hybridity on Australian screens. In C. Simpson, R. Murawska, & A. Lambert (Eds.), *Diaspora of Australian Cinema* (pp. 376-361). *Cultural Studies Review, 16*(2). Retrieved from http://epress.lib.uts.edu.au/journals/index.php/csrj/article/view/1708/1839

Krippendorff, K. (2013). *Content analysis: An introduction to its methodology.* (3rd ed.). Thousand Oaks, CA. SAGE Publication, Inc.

Kuper, A., Lingard, L., & Levinson, W. (2008). Critically appraising qualitative research. *British Medical Journal, 337*, 687-689. doi:10.1136/bmj.a1035

Love, M. C. (2010). The twilight of the pardon power. *Journal of Criminal Law & Criminology, 100*(3), 1169-1212. Retrieved from http://search.proquest.com/docview/848998384?accountid=35812

Mackenzie, I., & Smith, A. (2009). Deafness: The neglected and hidden disability. *Annals of Tropical Medicine & Parasitology. 103*(7), 1-7. doi: http://dx.doi.org/10.1179/000349809X12459740922372

Mandara, J., Varner, F., Greene, N., & Richman, S. (2009). Intergenerational family predictors of black-white achievement gap. *Journal of Educational Psychology, 101*(4), 867-878. doi: 10.1037/a0016644

Martin, R. E. (2012). Changing Staffing Patterns in Private and Public Research Universities (Working paper). doi: http://dx.doi.org/10.2139/ssrn.2012761

Matthews, L. E. (2005) Towards design of clarifying equity messages in mathematics reform. *The High School Journal, 88*(4), 46-58. Retrieved from http://search.proquest.com/docview/220230093?accountid=35812

Maxwell, B (2012). Make black male collegians the rule, not exception. *Sentinel & Enterprise,* pp. n/a. Retrieved from http://www.tampabay.com/opinion/columns/article1215901.ece

McCaskill, C. D. (2005). *The education of Black Deaf Americans in the 20th century: Policy implications for administrators in residential schools for the Deaf* (Doctoral dissertation). Retrieved from http://research.gallaudet.edu/Reports/details/380

McIntyre, E. (2007). Story discussion in the primary grades: Balancing authenticity and explicit teaching. *The Reading Teacher, 60*(7), 610- 620. Retrieved from http://search.proquest.com/docview/203287221?accountid=35812

McIntyre, E., Kyle, D. W., & Moore, G. H. (2006). A primary-grade teacher's guidance toward small-group dialogue. *Reading Research Quarterly, 41*(1), 36-66. doi: 10.1598/RRQ.41.1.2

Meadow-Orlans, K. P. (2001). Research and deaf education: Moving ahead while glancing back. *Journal of Deaf Studies and Deaf Education. 6*(2), 143- 148. doi: 10.1093/deafed/6.2.143

Mehra, S., Eavey, R. D., & Keamy, D. G. (2009). The epidemiology of hearing impairment in the United States: Newborns, children, and adolescents. *Ontolaryngology – Head and Neck Surgery, 140*(4), 461-472. doi: 10.1016/j.otohns.2008.12.022

Merton, R. K. (1948). The self-fulfilling prophecy. *Antioch Review, 8*, 193-210. Retrieved from http://www.jstor.org/stable/4609267

Meyer, N. J., & Munson, B. H. (2005). Personalizing and empowering environmental education through expressive writing. *The Journal of Environmental Education, 36*(3), 6-14. Retrieved from http://go.galegroup.com/ps/i.do?id=GALE%7CA134576192&v=2.1&u=wash75104&it=r&p=PROF&sw=w

Morgan, D. L. (2007). Paradigms lost and pragmatism regained: Methodological implications combining qualitative and quantitative methods. *Journal of Mixed Methods Research, 1*(1), 48-76. doi: 10.1177/2345678906292462

Müller-Merbach, H. (2007). Kant's two paths of knowledge creation: A priori versus a posteriori. *Knowledge Management Research & Practice, 5*(1), 64-65. doi:10.1057/palgrave.kmrp.8500123

Neuman, W. L. (2006). *Social research methods: Qualitative, and quantitative approaches.* (6th ed.). Boston, MA: Allyn and Bacon, Inc.

Nieto, S. (2009). *Language, culture, and teaching: Critical perspectives.* (2nd ed.). New York, NY: Routledge.

Ornstein, A. C., & Levine, D. U. (1989). Social class, race, and school achievement: Problems and prospects. *Journal of Teacher Education, 40*(5), 17-23. doi: 10.1177/002248718904000503

Oseguera, L. (2005-2006). Four- and six-year baccalaureate degree completion by institutional characteristics and racial/ethnic groups. *Journal of College Student Retention, 7*(1-2), 19-59. Retrieved from http://search.proquest.com/docview/196730632?accountid=35812

Padden, C., & Humphries, T. (1988). *Deaf in America: Voices from a culture.* Cambridge, MA: Harvard University Press.

Patton, J. M. (1998). The disproportionate representation of African Americans in special education: Looking behind the curtain for understanding and solutions. *The Journal of Special Education, 32*(1), 25-31. doi: 10.1177/002246699803200104

Pfeiffer, M. A., & Pfeiffer, K. T. (2011). School picture day and self-concept: A smile is worth the trouble. *Teaching Exceptional Children, 43*(3), 50-54. Retrieved from http://www.uaa.alaska.edu/sociology/upload/Pfeiffer2011_TEC.pdf

Pinkerton, K. (2010). College persistence of readers on the margin: A population overlooked. *Research & Teaching in Developmental Education, 27*(1), 20-31. Retrieved from http://search.proquest.com/docview/847387087?accountid=35812

Popp, D. (2005). *Meta-expectations: A theory of expectancy effects in social Interaction.* The University of Connecticut). *ProQuest Dissertations and Theses,* 172 p. http://search.proquest.com/docview/305011969?accountid=35812

Rao V., & Flores, G. (2007). Why aren't there more African-American physicians? A qualitative study and exploratory inquiry of African-American students' perspectives on careers in medicine. *Journal of the National Medical Association, 99*(9), 986-993. Retrieved from http://www.ncbi.nlm.nih.gov/pmc/articles/PMC2575862/

Renn, K. A. (2008). Research on biracial and multicultural identity development: Overview and synthesis. *New Directions for Student Services, 2008*(123), 13-21. doi: 10.1002/ss.282

Richardson, J. T. E., Marschark, M., Sarchet, T., & Sapere, P. (2010). Deaf and hard-of-hearing students' experiences in mainstream and separate postsecondary education. *Journal of Deaf Studies and Deaf Education, 15*(4), 358-382. doi: 10.1093/deafed/enq030

Riley, T., & Ungerleider, C. (2008). Preservice teachers' discriminatory judgments. *Alberta Journal of Educational Research, 54*(4), 378-387. Retrieved from http://ajer.synergiesprairies.ca/ajer/index.php/ajer/article/viewFile/651/632

Roessler, R. T., & Foshee, K. (2010). Impact of occupational instruction on the performance andvocational identity of special education students. *Rural Special Education Quarterly, 29*(3), 23-28. Retrieved from http://jaymeneal.wikispaces.com/file/view/article+2.pdf

Rolfe, G. (2006). Validity, trustworthiness and rigour: quality and the idea of qualitative research. *Journal of Advanced Nursing, 53*(3), 304-310. doi: 10.1111/j.1365-2648.2006.03727.x

Rowley, D. J., Lujan, H. D., & Dolence, M. G. (1997). *Strategic change in colleges and universities: Planning to survive and prosper.* San Francisco, CA: Jossey-Bass Publishers

Rosenthal, R., & Jacobson, L. (1968). *Pygmalion in the classroom: Teacher expectation and pupils' intellectual development.* New York, NY: Holt, Rinehart & Winston.

Rubie-Davies, C. M. (2010). Teacher expectations and perceptions of student attributes: Is there a relationship? *British Journal of Educational Psychology, 80*(1), 121-135. doi: 10.1348/000709909X466334

Rubie-Davies, C. M. (2006). Teacher expectations and student self-perceptions: Exploring relationships. *Psychology in the Schools, 43*(5), 537-552. doi: 10.1002/pits.20169

Rubie-Davies, C., Hattie, J., & Hamilton, R. (2006). Expecting the best for students: Teacher expectations and academic outcomes. *British Journal of Educational Psychology, 76,* 429-444. doi: 10.1348/000709905X53589

Rubie-Davies, C. M., Peterson, E., Irving, E., Widdowson, D., & Dixon, R. (2010). Expectations of achievement: Student, teacher and parent perceptions. *Research in Education 83*(1), 36-53. Retrieved from http://search.proquest.com/docview/759006886?accountid=27346

Salen, S. J., & Garrick Duhaney, L. M. (2005). Understanding and addressing the disproportionate representation of students of color in special education. *Intervention in School and Clinic, 40*(4), 213-221. Retrieved from http://search.proquest.com/docview/759006886?accountid=27346

Sanchez, R., & Sital, R. (2010). Tougher standards option good for students. *Tri-City Herald,* p. A7. Retrieved from http://proquest.umi.com

Sarant, J. Z., Holt, C. M., Dowell, R. C., Rickards, F. W., & Blamey, P. J. (2008). Spoken language development in oral preschool children with permanent childhood deafness. *Journal of Deaf Studies and Deaf Education, 14*(2), 205-217. doi: 10.1093/deafed/enn034

Scott, C. (2010). The status of education and its consequences for educational research: An anthropological exploration. *Australian Journal of Education, 54*(3), 325-340. Retrieved from http://search.proquest.com.ezproxy.apollolibrary.com/docview/819182720?accountid=35812

Scruggs, T. E., Mastropieri, M. A., & McDuffie, K. A. (2007). Co-teaching in inclusive classrooms: A metasynthesis of qualitative research. *Exceptional Children, 73*(4), 392-416. Retrieved from http://search.proquest.com/docview/201097061?accountid=35812

Sears, D. O. (2008). The American color line 50 years after *Brown v Board*: Many 'peoples of color' or black exceptionalism? In G. Adams, M. Biernat, N. R. Branscombe, C. S. Crandall, & L. S. Wrightsman (Eds.), *Commemorating Brown: The social psychology of racism and discrimination*, pp. 133-152. Washington, DC: APA Books.

Senge, P. M. (1990). *The fifth discipline: The art & practice of the learning organization*. New York, NY: Doubleday.

Shom, C. (2006). Minorities and the egalitarian-meritocratic values conflict in American higher education: New answers for an old problem. *Journal of College Admission, 190*, 8-13. doi: 10.1002/j.2161-1912.1991.tb00555.x

Sinkovics, R. R., Penz, E., & Ghauri, P. N. (2008). Enhancing the trustworthy of qualitative research in international business. *Management International Review, 48*(6), 689-713. doi: 10.1007/s11575-008-0103-z

Skiba, R. J., Simmons, A. B., Ritter, S., Gidd, A. C., Rausch, M. K., Cuadrado, J., & Chung, C. G. (2008). Achieving equity in special education: History, status, and current challenges. *Exceptional Children, 74*(3), 264-288. Retrieved from http://proxyga.wrlc.org:80/login?url=http://search.proquest.com/docview/201209818?accountid=27346

Smit, B., & Fritz, E. (2008). Understanding teacher identity from a symbolic interactionist perspective: Two ethnographic narratives. *South African Journal of Education, 28,* 91-101. Retrieved from http://www.scielo.org.za/scielo.php?pid=S0256-01002008000100006&script=sci_arttext

Stepchenkova, S., Kirilenko, A. P., & Morrison, A. M. (2009). Facilitating content analysis in tourism research. *Journal of Travel Research, 47*(4), 454-469. doi:10.1177/0047287508326509

Tauber, R. T. (1997). *Self-fulfilling prophecy: A practical guide to its use in education.* Westport, CT: Preager.

Tatum, B. D. (1997). *"Why are all the Black kids sitting together in the cafeteria?" and other conversations about race.* New York, NY: Basic Books.

Thomas, W. I. (1928). *The child in America: Behavior problems and programs.* New York, NY: Knopf.

Torres, V., Jones, S. R., & Renn, K. A. (2009). Identity development theories in student affairs origins, current status, and new approaches. *Journal of College Student Development, 5*(6), 577-596. Retrieved from https://www.msu.edu/~renn/TorresJonesRenn2009.pdf

Trochim, W. M. K., & Donnelly, J. P. (2008). *The research methods knowledge base.* Mason OH: Cengage Learning

Troiana, P. F., Liefeld, J. A., & Trachtenberg, J. V. (2010). Academic support and college success for postsecondary students with learning disabilities. *Journal of College Reading and Learning, 40*(2). 35-44. Retrieved from http://search.proquest.com/docview/340359580?accountid=27346

Tsiplakides, I., & Keramida, A. (2010). The relationship between teacher expectations and student achievement in the teaching of English as a foreign language. *English Language Teaching, 3*(2), 22-26. Retrieved from http://www.ccsenet.org/journal/index.php/elt/article/view/5347/4920

U.S. Department of Education. (2010). *National U.S. Department of Education.* Retrieved from http://nces.ed.gov

U.S. Department of Education. (2009). *The No Child Left Behind Act of 2002.* Retrieved from http://www.ed.gov/policy/elsec/guid/states/index.html

U.S. Department of Education. (2007). *Digest of Education Statistics.* Retrieved from http://www.mnyscherc.org/site/672/doc_library/2007%20Digest%20of%20Education%20Statistics.pdf

Usher, E. L. (2009). Sources of middle school students' self-efficacy in mathematics: A qualitative investigation. *American Educational Research Journal, 46*(1), 275-314. doi: 10.3102/0002831208324517

Van Cleve, J. V., & Crouch, B. (1989). *A place of their own: Creating the Deaf community in America.* Washington, D.C.: Gallaudet University Press.

White, M. D., & Marsh, E. E. (2006). Content analysis: A flexible methodology. *Library Trends, 55*(1), 22-45. doi: 10.1353/lib.2006.0053

Willard, J., Madon, S., Guyll, M., Spoth, R., & Jussim, L. (2008). Self-efficacy as a moderator of negative and positive self-fulfilling prophecy effects: Mothers' beliefs and children's alcohol use. *European Journal of Social Psychology, 38,* 499-520. doi: 10.1002/ejsp.429

Williamson, C. E. (2007). *Black deaf students: A model for educational success.* Washington, DC: Gallaudet University Press.

Wilson, M. A., & Stephens, D. E. (2007). Great expectations: An examination of the differences between high and low expectancy athletes' perception of coach treatment. *Journal of Sport Behavior, 30*(1), 358-373. Retrieved from http://findarticles.com/p/articles/mi_hb6401/is_3_30/ai_n29369178/

Wong, J. T. Y., & Hui, E. C. M. (2006). Research notes – power of expectations. *Property Management, 24*(5), 496-506. Doi: 10.1108/02637470610710547

Wooley, M. E., & Bowen, G. L. (2007). In the context of risk: Supportive adults and the school engagement of middle school students. *Family Relations, 56*(1), 92-104. doi: 10.1111/j.1741-3729.2007.00442.x

Appendix A

Informed Consent Letter

UNIVERSITY OF PHOENIX

INFORMED CONSENT: PARTICIPANTS 18 YEARS OF AGE AND OLDER

Dear Participant,
I am a student at the University of Phoenix working on a doctoral degree. I am conducting a research study entitled, "The impact of the self-fulfilling prophecy on Black Deaf male students." The purpose of this study is to explore the perceptions of differential treatments of Black Deaf male students in postsecondary setting to determine if the self-fulfilling prophecy theory contributed to their pedagogic achievements.

Your participation will involve completing an open-ended qualitative survey. **Participation in this study is voluntary. If you choose not to participate or to withdraw from the study at any time, you can do so without penalty or loss of benefit to yourself. In this research, there are no foreseeable risks to you.** You will be compensated $25 for your participation. The survey should take approximately twenty to thirty minutes or less to complete.

However, a possible benefit of your participation is information and awareness about the research topic and coping strategies in postsecondary environment for the participants. Another benefit is to give the participants an opportunity to give feedback to higher education administrators about the subject's postsecondary experience or lack of.

If you have any questions concerning the research study, please call me.

As a participant in this study, you should understand the following:

1. Your participation is voluntary.
2. You may decline to participate or withdraw from participation at any time without consequences.
3. Your identity will be kept strictly **confidential**.
4. The researcher has thoroughly explained the parameters of the research study and all of your questions and concerns have been addressed.
5. Data will be stored in a secure and locked area. The data will be held for a period of three years, and then destroyed.
6. The research results will be used for publication.

By signing this form you acknowledge that you understand the nature of the study, there is no potential risks to you as a participant, and the means by which your identity will be kept confidential. Your signature on this form also indicates that you are 18 years old or older and that you give your permission to voluntarily serve as a participant in the study described.

Signature of the interviewee _____ Date _____

Signature of the researcher _____ Date _____

Appendix B

Survey Questions

Instructions

Please read every question carefully and take a moment to reflect on your academic experience before you answer. Answer to the best of your recollection.

What is your perception of your college professor's expectations of your academic performance?

☐ My Professor set high expectations of my academic performance

☐ My Professor set low expectations of my academic performance

☐ My Professor set expectation, but they weren't too high or too low

☐ My Professor's expectations were not clear to me

☐ My Professor's expectations did not matter to me

☐ I set my own expectations of my academic performance

☐ Other, please describe_____

Please explain why you chose your answer
_____
_____
_____

How did your professor set expectations of you?

☐ My Professor told me privately that he or she expects me to pass his or her courses

☐ My Professor told my classmates and me of his or her expectation during class

☐ My Professor reminded my classmates and me of his or her expectations at every class

☐ My Professor did not tell me his or her expectation

☐ My Professor's expectations did not matter to me

☐ I set my own expectations of my academic performance

☐ Other, please describe_____

Please explain why you chose your answer
_____
_____
_____

How did your professor respond to you when you did not perform to his or her expectations?

☐ My Professor expressed disappointment verbally in a positive way and asked me to meet with him or her after class

☐ My Professor expressed his or her disappointment on my homework in a positive way and asked me to meet with him or her after class

☐ My Professor expressed his or her disappointment but did not follow up to see how I am doing

☐ My Professor never expressed his or her disappointment and I felt he or she didn't care about my academic performance

☐ My Professor's body language showed indifference towards me when I did not perform to expectations

☐ I cared about my education and worked hard to perform well in all my classes

☐ Other, please describe_____

Please explain why you chose your answer
_____
_____
_____

Provide examples of how your professor communicated expectations of you.

☐ My Professor made eye contact with me in class while communicating his or her expectations. That made me feel he or she cared

☐ My Professor met with me during his or her office hours to make sure I was clear about his or her expectations of me

☐ My Professor reminded us about expectations during every class

☐ My Professor did not communicate his or her expectations and I wasn't clear about the expectations of me

☐ I cared about my education and worked hard to perform well in all my classes and did not need the Professor's to set expectations of me

☐ Other, please describe_____

Please explain why you chose your answer
_____
_____

How did your professor respond to you when you performed above expectations?

☐ My Professor verbally gave me positive reinforcement and privately encouraged me to continue doing well

☐ My Professor wrote positive comments on my paper

☐ My Professor publicly praised my work in classroom and used me as an example to show his or her expectations

☐ My Professor did not respond when I performed above his or her expectation

☐ It was difficult to tell if my Professor was praising my work because he or she made general statements to the entire class

☐ I cared about my education and worked hard to perform well in all my classes and did not need the Professor's to encourage me

☐ Other, please describe_____

Please explain why you chose your answer
_____
_____
_____

Describe how your professor encouraged you to perform better than your classmates.

☐ My Professor publicly gave me positive feedback about my work in class

☐ My Professor gave me more homework for extra credit

☐ My Professor met with me frequently to help me clarify assignments

☐ My Professor did not give me any feedback about my work regardless of how well I did

☐ My Professor provided generic feedback to everyone in class

☐ I cared about my education and worked hard to perform well in all my classes and did not need the Professor's feedback

☐ Other, please describe_____

Please explain why you chose your answer

_____
_____
_____
_____

Describe an example showing that you succeeded academically because of your professor's expectations

☐ My Professor's reminders about expectations helped me succeed

☐ My Professor's one-on-one attention to my performance helped me succeed

☐ My Professor's verbal praise in class about my academic performance motivated me to succeed

☐ My Professor gave me additional homework that helped my academic performance

☐ My Professor provided encouraging words such as "Good job," or "Keep up the good work, I am proud of you."

☐ I cared about my education and worked hard to perform well in all my classes and did not need the Professor's feedback

☐ Other, please describe_____

Please explain why you chose your answer

_____
_____
_____

If applicable, provide an example showing that you failed academically because of your professor's expectations

☐ My Professor did not set any expectations of me

☐ My Professor and I did not discuss my performance

☐ My Professor did not give me verbal praise in class about my academic performance

☐ My Professor did not give me additional homework to help academic performance

☐ My Professor often shared discouraging words with me about my performance

☐ I cared about my education but my Professor didn't seem to care at all

☐ Other, please describe_____

Please explain why you chose your answer

_____
_____
_____

Share examples of where professor set expectations that *positively* influenced your classroom performance.

☐ The Professor told the class about his or her expectation and thoroughly discussed the syllabus

☐ The Professor gave homework and collected them equally from the class

☐ The Professor publicly gave verbal praise to my classmates and me when we performed above his or her expectations

☐ The Professor encouraged my classmates and me to take advantage of his or her office hours for tutoring

☐ The Professor was equally attentive to my classmates and I during class

☐ The Professor called upon me when I raised my hand in class. I did not feel ignored

☐ The Professor probed me for more information when I answered a question in class

Please explain why you chose your answer
___
___
___

Share examples where professor set expectations that *negatively* influenced your classroom performance?

☐ The Professor did not tell my classmates and me about his or her expectation but distributed the syllabus

☐ The Professor sometimes did not ask me for my homework

☐ The Professor publicly scolded me when I did not perform well in class

☐ The Professor was not forthcoming about office hours and was often not there for me when I went to see him or her

☐ The Professor often said, "Don't worry about that" when I requested help

☐ The Professor did not call upon me when I raised my hand in class, choosing to respond to other classmates instead.

☐ The Professor probed another classmate when I got the answer wrong and stopped calling upon me to answer questions

Please explain why you chose your answer
___
___
___

What class activities did the professor use to help you succeed in class?

☐ The Professor put me on a team with my classmates to work on class assignments together and checked to make sure I participated

☐ The Professor called upon me to answer questions and probed me for answers even when I didn't raise my hand

☐ The Professor called on me to help other classmates and gave us verbal praise even when we couldn't answer

☐ The Professor announced special assignments and named me group leader

☐ The Professor often asked me to solve problems on the blackboard, which was common for other classmates as well

☐ The Professor maintained eye contact and smiled at me all the time in class when he or she probed for answers from me

☐ The Professor gave pop quizzes to help us maintain good grades in class

Please explain why you chose your answer
_____
_____
_____

What class activities did the professor use to help you feel academically challenged?

☐ The Professor put me on a team with my classmates for class assignments and made sure I participated

☐ The Professor called upon me to answer questions and probed me for answers even when I didn't raise my hand

☐ The Professor called on me to help other classmates in class and gave us verbal praise even when we couldn't answer

☐ The Professor announced special assignments and named me as group leader

☐ The Professor often asked me to solve problems on the blackboard, which was common for all my classmates

☐ The Professor maintained eye contact and smiled at me all the time in class when probing for answers from me

☐ The Professor gave pop quizzes to help us maintain good grades

Please explain why you chose your answer
_____
_____
_____

Give an example of how the professor's feedback encouraged you to succeed in the classroom.

☐ The Professor gave me verbal and written feedback about my assignments

- [ ] The Professor was consistent with feedback
- [ ] The Professor publicly gave me feedback about my work during team and individual activities
- [ ] The Professor publicly cited my work as an example for others to follow
- [ ] The Professor asked me for permission to post my work for other classmates to use as an example
- [ ] The Professor told me in class and/or during meetings that I was a good student
- [ ] The Professor recommended my name for course-related panels and special events

Please explain why you chose your answer

_____
_____
_____

Provide an example of how professor's feedback discouraged you that led you to fail.

- [ ] The Professor did not give me feedback on my homework. He or she only wrote the grade with no further information.
- [ ] The Professor publicly disciplined me in class when I made a mistake
- [ ] The Professor gave me low grades even when I worked really hard
- [ ] The Professor said out loud that I was "wrong" when I gave an answer but did not do that with my classmates
- [ ] The Professor was often indifferent towards me and did not smile at me in class
- [ ] The Professor often told me to get help because my work was not acceptable, but did not ask me to stop by his or her office for help
- [ ] The Professor often completely ignored my questions in class

Please explain why you chose your answer

_____
_____
_____

Describe an example that indicates the professor cared about your classroom learning

- [ ] The Professor greeted me before class and asked me how I was doing on my assignments
- [ ] The Professor publicly used me as an example of a model student
- [ ] The Professor provided extra readings or work that were not related to class

☐ The Professor asked me to stop by his or her office when he or she noticed something might be wrong based on my assignment quality

☐ The Professor introduced me to other Professors and said nice things about me

☐ The Professor shared information that he or she felt would help my academic career such as special presentations on and off-campus

☐ The Professor always reminded me that if I needed anything at all for school, to see him or her for assistance

Please explain why you chose your answer
_____
_____
_____

Appendix C

Collaboration Letter

Date: Xxxxxx

To: Office of the Provost/Institutional Review Board
University of Phoenix

This letter acknowledges that

___Xxxxxxxxxxxxxxxxx____ is collaborating with
   (Name of the agency)

___Xxxxxxxxxxxxx_____
   (Name of the student)

enrolled in the Doctor in Organizational Leadership and Management program at the University of Phoenix in conducting the

proposed research. We understand the purpose of this research

is to explore the perceptions of a purposive sample of Black Deaf male students in postsecondary setting in Washington, D.C. to determine if the SFP theory contributed to their pedagogic achievement,

and will be conducted under the supervision of Xxxxxxxxxxxxxx
                                                (Faculty Name).

This project will be an integral part of our institution/agency and will be conducted as a collaborative effort and will be part of our curriculum/research/data/service delivery model.

Sincerely,

Xxxxxxxxxxxxxxxxx
(Representative Collaborating Institution/Agency)

Appendix D

Payment Form

Compensation From

Dear participant,

Thank you for participating in this survey. Please check how you would like to be compensated and then return this form with the completed survey in the self-addressed envelope. Please email me with questions.

Thank you again for your cooperation and participation.

Name:

Address:

☐ American Express Gift Card

Appendix E

Recruitment Poster

School of Advanced Studies - University of Phoenix Online

BLACK DEAF MALE PARTICIPANTS NEEDED FOR RESEARCH IN

THE SELF-FULFILLING PROPHECY

We are looking for Black Deaf Male student volunteers to participate in a study:
The Impact of the Self-fulfilling prophecy on Black Deaf Male Students

As a participant in this study, you would be asked to:

Complete a 20 to 30 minutes or less survey about factors that influence your college experience and expectations that influence your academic achievement.

In appreciation for your time, you will receive
A $XX Dollars American Express Gift Card

For more information about this study, or to volunteer for this study,
please contact: Primary researcher
School of Advance Studies – University of Phoenix Online

This study has been reviewed by Institutional Review

Appendix F

Invitation Letter

April 11, 2011

Dear Potential Study Participant:

I am a doctoral candidate at the University of Phoenix working on a Doctor of leadership and management degree. As a doctoral dissertation research project, I am conducting a research study entitled: The impact of the self-fulfilling prophecy on Black Deaf Male students. Participating in this research is voluntary and will entail completing an individual survey that should last approximately one (1) hour or less about your perceptions in the postsecondary setting.

Remember, participation is voluntary and you may chose to withdraw your participation at any time. If you chose to withdraw, you can send me an email, call me via videophone, or text me. I will be happy to remove you from the list of participant immediately without any penalty to you. You have my utmost respect and confidence about the decision to withdraw.

Participants must be 18 years of age or older Black, Deaf and male who are attending or attended a postsecondary institution in Washington, DC. Please be assured that after the initial contact, your name will be discarded, shredded if it was written or printed, and destroyed to ensure complete confidentiality. When the result of the research study is published, your name will not be used and your results will remain confidential.

This research will not pose any foreseeable risks to you, as the focus will be on your perceptions of your academic experience in the postsecondary setting. This study may not benefit you directly, however it might help to identify some coping strategies to help current and future Black Deaf male students in the postsecondary setting. It is hopeful that those strategies will help current and future Black Deaf males' progress to graduation to narrow the achievement gap.

After you have read this invitation letter, you have to sign the informed consent form (Attachment A) prior to completing the survey (Attachment B). When you complete the survey, please enclose it in the self-addressed envelope and send it back. Once I receive your survey I will immediately send you the $25 in the manner that you indicated on the payment form (Attachment G). If you have any questions regarding this research study, or if you know someone else who fits the study criteria, please email me.

Sincerely,

Primary researcher

Appendix G

Alumni Recruitment Email Advertisement

School of Advanced Studies - University of Phoenix Online

BLACK DEAF MALE ALUMNI

PARTICIPANTS NEEDED FOR RESEARCH IN

THE SELF-FULFILLING PROPHECY

We are looking for Black Deaf Male alumni volunteers who graduated between 2002 and 2009 to participate in a study:

The Impact of the Self-fulfilling prophecy on Black Deaf Male Students

As a participant in this study, you would be asked to:

Complete a 30 minutes or less survey about factors that influence your college experience and expectations that influence your academic achievement.

In appreciation for your time, you will receive
A $XX Dollars American Express Gift Card

For more information about this study, or to volunteer for this study, please contact: Primary researcher
School of Advance Studies – University of Phoenix Online

This study has been reviewed by Institutional Review

Appendix H

Tables

Table 15

Teacher Forms Expectations Questions

R1	SFP step 1	SQ
How do Black Deaf male students perceive a teacher's expectations of their academic performances in postsecondary institutions	Teacher forms expectations	How did your professor set expectations of you? Share examples of where professors set expectations that *positively* influenced your classroom performance. Share examples where professors set expectations that *negatively* influenced your classroom performance?

Note. R1 = Research Question 1; SFP = self-fulfilling prophecy; SQ = Survey Question

Table 16

Differential Manner Questions

R2	SFP step 2	SQ
How do Black Deaf male students perceive teacher expectations influence on their achievements?	Based upon these expectations, the teacher acts in a differential manner	What is your perception of your college professor's expectations of your academic performance? Provide examples of how your professor communicated expectations of you. Describe an example that indicates the professor cared about your classroom learning.

Note. R = Research Question 2; SFP = self-fulfilling prophecy; SQ = Survey Question

Table 17

Behaviors and Achievement Questions

R2	SFP step 3	SQ
How do Black Deaf male students perceive teacher expectations influence on their achievements?	The teacher's treatment tells each student what behaviors and achievement the teacher expects	Provide an example of how the professor's feedback discouraged you that led you to fail. How did your professor respond to you when you did not perform to his or her expectations?

Note. R = Research Question 2; SFP = self-fulfilling prophecy; SQ = Survey Question

Table 18

Consistent Treatment Questions

R2	SFP step 4	SQ
How do Black Deaf male students perceive teacher expectations influence on their achievements?	If the treatment is consistent over time, and if the student does not actively resist, it will tend to shape his or her behavior and achievement	Give an example of how the professor's feedback encouraged you to succeed in the classroom. What class activities did the professor use to help you succeed in class? How did your professor respond to you when you performed above expectations? Describe an example of how your professor encouraged you to perform better than your classmates.

Note. R = Research Question 2; SFP = self-fulfilling prophecy; SQ = Survey Question

Table 19

Conform to Expectation Questions

R2	SFP step 5	SQ
How do Black Deaf male students perceive teacher expectations influence on their achievements?	With time, the student's behavior and achievement will conform more closely to that expected of him or her	What class activities did the professor use to help you succeed in class? If applicable, provide an example showing that you failed academically because of your professor's expectations. Describe an example showing that you succeeded academically because of your professor's expectations.

Note. R = Research Question 2; SFP = self-fulfilling prophecy; SQ = Survey Question

Table 20

Teacher Expectation Participants

SQ	UG responses *n=10*	AL responses *n=10*
How did your professor set expectations of you?	My Professor told me privately that he or she expects me to pass his or her courses	My Professor told me privately that he or she expects me to pass his or her courses
	My Professor told me privately that he or she expects me to pass his or her courses	My Professor told my classmates and me of his or her expectation during class
	My Professor told me privately that he or she expects me to pass his or her courses	My Professor told my classmates and me of his or her expectation during class
	My Professor told my classmates and me of his or her expectation during class	My Professor told my classmates and me of his or her expectation during class
	My Professor told my classmates and me of his or her expectation during class	My Professor told my classmates and me of his or her expectation during class
	My Professor told my classmates and me of his or her expectation during class	My Professor told my classmates and me of his or her expectation during class
	My Professor told my classmates and me of his or her expectation during class	My Professor told my classmates and me of his or her expectation during class
	My Professor reminded my classmates and me of his or her expectations at every class	My Professor told my classmates and me of his or her expectation during class
	My Professor reminded my classmates and me of his or her expectations at every class	My Professor's expectations did not matter to me
	I set my own expectations of my academic performance	I set my own expectations of my academic performance

Note. SQ = Survey Question; UG = Undergraduates participants; AL = Alumni participants

Table 20a

Illuminations: Teacher expectations

SQ	UG Comments (*n*=10)	AL Comments (*n*=10)
How did your professor set expectations of you?	• My professor told us that we can pass the class if we do what asked • Through shared experience • Syllabus • I paid the courses so I have to do well in school. My responsibility, my choice, my decision • He want us to be equal and pass this course. He would like to see us graduate • Through private discussions and notes of papers after being graded • Because professor encourage the students understand what is important for your future. Expectation with goal is very important • My photographer teacher want the best of me	• Expectations were on just about every syllabus. However, when it came to grading the syllabus & expectations weren't always followed. • One professor was good at it. She mentioned about it every class. • Most of my professors made it clear to everyone in class what is expected of them during class. I don't recall ever being called in to any professor's office for private discussion of what this particular professor expect of me except for discussions of some of my work performances. • Professors would explain/told their expectations during the class. I felt they apply to everyone. • During Gallaudet years, I set my own expectations to achieve my academic performances regardless of my professors' expectations because I had goals to complete & follow the instruction to meet academic goals to obtain a degree. • That's because the professor would like to prove other students that I can do it better in the classroom • Standard procedure for all the students to get and complete tasks • Because I accept their attitude when I should have establish my expectation • She want me to success and had high expectation on me

Note. SQ = Survey Question; UG = Undergraduates participants; AL = Alumni participants

Table 21

Positive Expectations Participants

SQ	UG responses $n=10$	AL responses $n=10$
Share examples of where professors set expectations that *positively* influenced your classroom performance.	The Professor told the class about his or her expectation and thoroughly discussed the syllabus	The Professor told the class about his or her expectation and thoroughly discussed the syllabus
	The Professor told the class about his or her expectation and thoroughly discussed the syllabus	The Professor told the class about his or her expectation and thoroughly discussed the syllabus
	The Professor gave homework and collected them equally from the class	The Professor publicly gave verbal praise to my classmates and me when we performed above his or her expectations
	The Professor gave homework and collected them equally from the class	The Professor publicly gave verbal praise to my classmates and me when we performed above his or her expectations
	The Professor gave homework and collected them equally from the class	The Professor publicly gave verbal praise to my classmates and me when we performed above his or her expectations
	The Professor gave homework and collected them equally from the class	The Professor publicly gave verbal praise to my classmates and me when we performed above his or her expectations
	The Professor gave homework and collected them equally from the class	The Professor encouraged my classmates and me to take advantage of his or her office hours for tutoring
	The Professor gave homework and collected them equally from the class	The Professor encouraged my classmates and me to take advantage of his or her office hours for tutoring
	The Professor encouraged my classmates and me to take advantage of his or her office hours for tutoring	The Professor called upon me when I raised my hand in class. I did not feel ignored
	The Professor was equally attentive to my classmates and I during class	The Professor probed me for more information when I answered a question in class

Note. SQ = Survey Question; UG = Undergraduates participants; AL = Alumni participants

Table 21a

Annotations: Positive Expectations

SQ	UG Comments ($n=10$)	AL Comments ($n=10$)
Share examples of where professor set expectations that *positively* influenced your classroom performance.	• The Professor told the class about his or her expectation and thoroughly discussed the syllabus and The Professor encouraged my classmates and me to take advantage of his or her office hours for tutoring • Professors made themselves available at all timer • That has always helped me perform better. A professor who does not show favoritism • Nice of the professor • He want to be fair with us • Seeing how professor's communicate with the class in its entirety makes the difference for me • Because they just want to make sure all students collected homework equally from the class • Because it help me remind the homework or through syllabus	• A psychology professor expressed how he truly enjoyed reading an end of the year papers and pulled me to the side and personally stated he enjoyed mine. He asked me to share it w/ some of his colleagues & the class. • More attention, more motivated • Verbal praises to everyone from the professor may have positively influenced my classroom performance but its really my hard work that makes a difference • Professor treat their students equally; will feel included and not singling me out. • I follow what were needed to achieve my academic goals • The more I raised my hand in class, the more I'll get incentive or motivated to work hard in the class • It like played by the book. Because I know when to do the work in time management • She have high expectation for us and want to share our work

Note. SQ = Survey Question; UG = Undergraduates participants; AL = Alumni participants

Table 22

Negative Expectations Participants

SQ	UG responses $n=10$	AL responses $n=10$
Share examples where professors set expectations that *negatively* influenced your classroom performance?	The Professor did not tell my classmates and me about his or her expectation but distributed the syllabus	The Professor did not tell my classmates and me about his or her expectation but distributed the syllabus
	The Professor did not tell my classmates and me about his or her expectation but distributed the syllabus	The Professor did not tell my classmates and me about his or her expectation but distributed the syllabus
	No answer	No answer
	The Professor sometimes did not ask me for my homework	The Professor was not forthcoming about office hours and was often not there for me when I went to see him or her
	The Professor publicly scolded me when I did not perform well in class	No answer
	The Professor was not forthcoming about office hours and was often not there for me when I went to see him or her	No answer
	The Professor often said, "Don't worry about that" when I requested help	The Professor often said, "Don't worry about that" when I requested help
	The Professor often said, "Don't worry about that" when I requested help	No answer
	N/A	The Professor did not call upon me when I raised my hand in class, choosing to respond to other classmates instead.
	The Professor probed another classmate when I got the answer wrong and stopped calling upon me to answer questions	The Professor probed another classmate when I got the answer wrong and stopped calling upon me to answer questions

Note. SQ = Survey Question; UG = Undergraduates participants; AL = Alumni participants

Table 22a

Elucidations: Negative Expectations

SQ	UG Comments (*n*=10)	AL Comments (*n*=10)
Share examples where professor set expectations that *negatively* influenced your classroom performance.	• There was the one who would do that. So hated it • Professor just did not care, it seemed • Nothing • He was sometime mean when I tried to get more help • I like it when professor's are up front about their expectations • Because sometime I don't realize to turn in my homework in the class that I have homework on my hand • Because sometime I caused confusing	• I felt "INVISIBLE" to a professor who continuously called on my White counterparts and not me in one class. Classic example of White privilege was practiced in that class. However, I did not let if affect my academics but it could have easily done so. I cannot help but to wonder how many others experienced this and did not make it through. Racism as its BEST. • N/A It was because basketball program that adversely impact my classroom performance. KTP should have been around before I enrolled in 2002 • None of these responses applies to me. My negative classroom performance is because I didn't do my best. • No set expectations of a class; clueless • I felt that professor expected me to fix the problem on my own without asking for assistance from professor • Noticed when I answered the question wrong my professor would look for other classmate often professor chose White students instead of black students • For English field I ask to be pushed to understand what house or what not. So that I can prep for real world level

Note. SQ = Survey Question; UG = Undergraduates participants; AL = Alumni participants

Table 23

Statistics: Teacher expectations

SQ	UG Responses (*n*=10)	AL Responses (*n*=10)
How did your professor set expectations of you?	4 during class 3 in private 2 use reminders 1 set own expectations	7 during class 1 in private 1 set own expectation 1 didn't matter
Share examples of where the professor set expectations that *positively* influenced your classroom performance.	6 used homework 2 used syllabus 1 used office hours 1 equal attention to all	4 public praise 2 used syllabus 2 used office hours 1 individual attention 1 used probing
Share examples where the professor set expectations that *negatively* influenced your classroom performance.	2 did not set expectations 2 didn't worry about it 1 didn't ask for homework 1 public scolding 1 unclear office hours, unavailable during office hours 1 wrong answer? Probed another 1 N/A 1 no answer	2 did not set expectations 1 don't worry about it 1 raised hand and picked another 1 unclear office hours, unavailable during office hours 1 wrong answer? Probed another 4 no answer

Note. SQ = Survey Question; UG = Undergraduates participants; AL = Alumni participants

Table 24

Differential Treatment Participants

SQ	UG responses *n*=10	AL responses *n*=10
What is your perception of your college professor's expectations of your academic performance?	My Professor set high expectations of my academic performance	My Professor set high expectations of my academic performance
	My Professor set high expectations of my academic performance	My Professor set high expectations of my academic performance
	My Professor set high expectations of my academic performance	My Professor set low expectations of my academic performance
	My Professor set high expectations of my academic performance	My Professor set expectation, but they weren't too high or too low
	My Professor set high expectations of my academic performance	My Professor set expectation, but they weren't too high or too low
	My Professor set high expectations of my academic performance	My Professor set expectation, but they weren't too high or too low
	My Professor set high expectations of my academic performance	My Professor set expectation, but they weren't too high or too low
	My Professor set high expectations of my academic performance	I set my own expectations of my academic performance
	My Professor set expectation, but they weren't too high or too low	I set my own expectations of my academic performance
	My Professor set expectation, but they weren't too high or too low	I set my own expectations of my academic performance

Note. SQ = Survey Question; UG = Undergraduates participants; AL = Alumni participants

Table 24a

Rationalizations: Perception of Expectations

SQ	UG Comments (*n*=10)	AL Comments (*n*=10)
What is your perception of your college professor's expectations of your academic performance?	• Because it college and was suppose to learn things we never learn before • Because they always believed in my ability(ies) • The quality of work I turn in and my involvement, I believe • Teachers expect me to do well so I prove them wrong • Because he wanted me to be successful • Because of my life experiences • Because when you graduate from college you would learn what professor's expectation and prepare well • The classes weren't challenged enough I already learned it before	• I could easily read the majority of my professors whom did not know me well. They basically target AWAY from me while directing most of the attention to the majority of my White peers. I was somewhat INVISIBLE. • Higher Standard • Most of my professors in a lot of my classes have established guideline of how they expect us to perform during class but they weren't established to encourage specific students to excel beyond average in class • Because of my K-12 experience I decided to set expectations for myself. Held to my standards and be accountable. • I felt that professor was trying to be simply fair to me and other students to pass the course not same as hearing student at any university • I chose to set my own expectation of my academic performance because I can't expect my professor's expectation of my academic. Professors teach many students which I can't rely. I have my own academic goals is to complete my college degree. • They gave me the paper to follow that standard procedure so that I can either pass it or not. • Teachers/professors assume that I am setting my goal to go pros basketball so, they just want me to go through "motion" to fit in. • We (African American) need more role models to graduate from college and expect them to stay out of the street.

Note. SQ = Survey Question; UG = Undergraduates participants; AL = Alumni participants

Table 25

Communication of Expectation Participants

SQ	UG responses $n=10$	AL responses $n=10$
Provide examples of how your professor communicated expectations of you.	My Professor made eye contact with me in class while communicating his or her expectations. That made me feel he or she cared	My Professor made eye contact with me in class while communicating his or her expectations. That made me feel he or she cared
	My Professor made eye contact with me in class while communicating his or her expectations. That made me feel he or she cared	My Professor made eye contact with me in class while communicating his or her expectations. That made me feel he or she cared
	My Professor made eye contact with me in class while communicating his or her expectations. That made me feel he or she cared	My Professor made eye contact with me in class while communicating his or her expectations. That made me feel he or she cared
	My Professor made eye contact with me in class while communicating his or her expectations. That made me feel he or she cared	My Professor made eye contact with me in class while communicating his or her expectations. That made me feel he or she cared
	My Professor made eye contact with me in class while communicating his or her expectations. That made me feel he or she cared	My Professor reminded us about expectations during every class
	My Professor made eye contact with me in class while communicating his or her expectations. That made me feel he or she cared	My Professor reminded us about expectations during every class
	My Professor met with me during his or her office hours to make sure I was clear about his or her expectations of me	I cared about my education and worked hard to perform well in all my classes and did not need the Professor's to set expectations of me
	My Professor met with me during his or her office hours to make sure I was clear about his or her expectations of me	I cared about my education and worked hard to perform well in all my classes and did not need the Professor's to set expectations of me
	My Professor met with me during his or her office hours to make sure I was clear about his or her expectations of me	I cared about my education and worked hard to perform well in all my classes and did not need the Professor's to set expectations of me
	My Professor reminded us about expectations during every class	Other, please describe-

Note. SQ = Survey Question; UG = Undergraduates participants; AL = Alumni participants

Table 25a

Undertones: Communicating of Expectations

SQ	UG Comments (*n*=10)	AL Comments (*n*=10)
Provide examples of how your professor communicated expectations of you.	• They asked questions to make sure I understand • My professor met with me during his or her office hours to make sure I was clear about his or her expectations of me • Because I made sure my professor and I stay on same page • Often times I would request to meet with the professor, or he or she would remind me of his/her office hours. There we could talk about my subpar performance and how it could improve • Being supportive is helpful • Again, open dialogue • Because communication is key to avoid the forgettable	• At one point I set expectation of myself & met w/my life coach weekly to track that progress. My program at that point didn't matter as long as I was passing. • Professors always remain neutral • I recalled that expectations were established but weren't specific enough to target students to excel beyond average so if anything, they were reminded to everyone during class. • They would explain their expectations and sometimes give examples, but not all the time (examples). • Communication through email & in the office's hours • I felt that professor wanted to see me to do well in the class for the whole semester if I wish to meet the expectation • Same as above. Some of my professors met with me after class or met at his or her office hours to discuss about my academic performance. I had set my own expectation and cared about my academic so if I didn't do well I met with my professor asked for advice or feedback as to what I need to improve. • Some teachers care about what I do in projects and teamwork. Some just let me on the loop again and again when I don't know which one I did wrong. • Most of my professor wait later when I am passing or failing • When I need her, she always made eye contact to make sure I pay attention.

Note. SQ = Survey Question; UG = Undergraduates participants; AL = Alumni participants

Table 26

Classroom Learning Participants

SQ	UG responses *n*=10	AL responses *n*=10
Describe an example that indicates the professor cared about your classroom learning.	The Professor greeted me before class and asked me how I was doing on my assignments	The Professor greeted me before class and asked me how I was doing on my assignments
	The Professor greeted me before class and asked me how I was doing on my assignments	The Professor greeted me before class and asked me how I was doing on my assignments
	The Professor greeted me before class and asked me how I was doing on my assignments	The Professor greeted me before class and asked me how I was doing on my assignments
	The Professor greeted me before class and asked me how I was doing on my assignments	The Professor publicly used me as an example of a model student
	The Professor publicly used me as an example of a model student	The Professor asked me to stop by his or her office when he or she noticed something might be wrong based on my assignment quality
	The Professor asked me to stop by his or her office when he or she noticed something might be wrong based on my assignment quality	The Professor asked me to stop by his or her office when he or she noticed something might be wrong based on my assignment quality
	The Professor asked me to stop by his or her office when he or she noticed something might be wrong based on my assignment quality	The Professor introduced me to other Professors and said nice things about me
	The Professor introduced me to other Professors and said nice things about me	The Professor shared information that he or she felt would help my academic career such as special presentations on and off-campus
	The Professor shared information that he or she felt would help my academic career such as special presentations on and off-campus	No answer
	The Professor always reminded me that if I needed anything at all for school, to see him or her for assistance	The Professor always reminded me that if I needed anything at all for school, to see him or her for assistance

Note. SQ = Survey Question; UG = Undergraduates participants; AL = Alumni participants

Table 26a

Observations: Classroom Learning

SQ	UG Comments ($n=10$)	AL Comments ($n=10$)
Describe an example that indicates the professor cared about your classroom learning.	• Always a plus when they showed they cared • This is related to the high expectations thing when I was not performing well. The professor automatically knew something was wrong. • Empathy, understanding, easy to get along with me • He is always checking on me before classes • Sharing of information that would help my academic environment in and out of class • Because example is helpful know	• Networking was a weakness of mine, but one psychology professor took a ton of interest in me before he retired. He often introduced me to other professors & told me about opportunities to ... I wish I majored in psychology after I met him and wish I met him earlier. • I believe from time to time the professor tried to make sure I'm ok with assignments to show that he/she cares but I believe this was done to everyone else to promote fairness in class. • Taken interest in my performance; want me to succeed. And willing to take the time to help me. • Professors were inquiring me how I did with homework's - in caring approaches • That's because the professor had a heart for me to see if I'm having any problems or questions that UI need to address urgently. • So that all the student can learn better • After I proved my academically success • She always in positive environment when I approach her

Note. SQ = Survey Question; UG = Undergraduates participants; AL = Alumni participants

Table 27

Data: Differential Treatment

SQ	UG Responses (*n*=10)	AL Responses (*n*=10)
What is your perception of your college professor's expectations of your academic performance?	8 high expectations 2 not too high or too low	2 high expectations 4 not too high or too low 3 set own expectations 1 low expectation
Provide examples of how your professor's communicated expectations of you.	6 eye contact showed caring 3 office hours 1 reminder in class	4 eye contact showed caring 2 reminder during class 3 cared about own education 1 Other: eye contact with all
Describe an example that indicates the professor cared about your classroom learning	4 acknowledgement/inquiry 2 office hours/counseling 1 used as an example for others 1 introduced to other faculty 1 shared helpful tips 1 reminder/available to assist	3 acknowledgement/inquiry 2 office hours/counseling 1 used as an example for others 1 introduced to other faculty 1 shared helpful tips 1 reminder/available to assist

Note. SQ = Survey Question; UG = Undergraduates participants; AL = Alumni participants

Table 28

Behavior and Achievement Participants

SQ	UG responses $n=10$	AL responses $n=10$
Provide an example of how the professor's feedback discouraged you that led you to fail.	The Professor did not give me feedback on my homework. He or she only wrote the grade with no further information.	The Professor did not give me feedback on my homework. He or she only wrote the grade with no further information.
	The Professor did not give me feedback on my homework. He or she only wrote the grade with no further information.	No answer
	The Professor did not give me feedback on my homework. He or she only wrote the grade with no further information.	The Professor publicly disciplined me in class when I made a mistake
	The Professor did not give me feedback on my homework. He or she only wrote the grade with no further information.	The Professor gave me low grades even when I worked really hard
	The Professor did not give me feedback on my homework. He or she only wrote the grade with no further information.	The Professor gave me low grades even when I worked really hard
	The Professor publicly disciplined me in class when I made a mistake	The Professor said out loud that I was "wrong" when I gave an answer but did not do that with my classmates
	The Professor gave me low grades even when I worked really hard	The Professor often told me to get help because my work was not acceptable, but did not ask me to stop by his or her office for help
	No answer	No answer
	The Professor often told me to get help because my work was not acceptable, but did not ask me to stop by his or her office for help	No answer
	The Professor often completely ignored my questions in class	No answer

Note. SQ = Survey Question; UG = Undergraduates participants; AL = Alumni participants

Table 28a

Commentaries: Discouraging Feedback

SQ	UG Comments (*n*=10)	AL Comments (*n*=10)
Provide an example of how professor's feedback discouraged you that led you to fail.	• Perhaps because I knew the answer • How can I make any progress if I don't know what I did wrong • Nothing, This professor just know that I will do better • He is being more positive on me when I made mistakes and he is always same person to me • It's nice when they let you know why its wrong • Because sometime there is no feedback wish some professor should know my weakness	• Never. I only failed one course through my academic career and I take full responsibility for it. • N/A Nope. It was basketball coach's feedback that discouraged me that led me to fail. No study table for basketball program during my time. • Because I'm not perfect, there are times when I've received low grades for work I believed I placed my 100% effort unto. This might have contributed me to fail but I often felt that my failure is my responsibility. • No feedback make me feel the teacher doesn't care about me. That only applies for low/failing grades. But high grades, like a rubber stamp - good job. No positive comments or anything. • That's because the professor wasn't able to see my motivation to work hard on the test or assignments • To ensure that I improve my work ethic • NA because she always want me to pass

Note. SQ = Survey Question; UG = Undergraduates participants; AL = Alumni participants

Table 29

Defied Expectation Participants

SQ	UG responses *n*=10	AL responses *n*=10
How did your professor respond to you when you did not perform to his or her expectations?	My Professor expressed disappointment verbally in a positive way and asked me to meet with him or her after class	My Professor expressed disappointment verbally in a positive way and asked me to meet with him or her after class
	My Professor expressed disappointment verbally in a positive way and asked me to meet with him or her after class	My Professor expressed disappointment verbally in a positive way and asked me to meet with him or her after class
	My Professor expressed disappointment verbally in a positive way and asked me to meet with him or her after class	My Professor expressed his or her disappointment on my homework in a positive way and asked me to meet with him or her after class
	My Professor expressed disappointment verbally in a positive way and asked me to meet with him or her after class	My Professor expressed his or her disappointment on my homework in a positive way and asked me to meet with him or her after class
	My Professor expressed his or her disappointment on my homework in a positive way and asked me to meet with him or her after class	My Professor expressed his or her disappointment but did not follow up to see how I am doing
	My Professor expressed his or her disappointment on my homework in a positive way and asked me to meet with him or her after class	My Professor expressed his or her disappointment but did not follow up to see how I am doing
	My Professor expressed his or her disappointment on my homework in a positive way and asked me to meet with him or her after class	My Professor expressed his or her disappointment but did not follow up to see how I am doing
	My Professor expressed his or her disappointment but did not follow up to see how I am doing	My Professor's body language showed indifference towards me when I did not perform to expectations
	N/A	I cared about my education and worked hard to perform well in all my classes
	I cared about my education and worked hard to perform well in all my classes	I cared about my education and worked hard to perform well in all my classes

Note. SQ = Survey Question; UG = Undergraduates participants; AL = Alumni participants

Table 29a

Accounts: Defied Expectations

SQ	UG Comments (*n*=10)	AL Comments (*n*=10)
How did your professor respond to you when you did not perform to his or her expectations?	• This is what my professor does to me when I am not doing my work • They did this to help me improve • Through email or private meetings. If I was not performing up to par my professor would always show concern • Its an example of role model • He expected me to understand clearly • I tend to develop relationships w/ my teachers to the point of open dialogue and discussion • Because sometime often when I was confused so my chance to teacher during office hour to discuss with concern • I never disappointment	• I felt even at the graduate level when I didn't do something the way THEY wanted it done it was almost as if I might AS well have died. They had limited office hours and was tough to meet with them and I didn't feel comfortable asking for help after the first meeting because of their nonchalant attitude. • They see students as inventories • I don't recall having a lot of issues with not meeting the professor's established expectations. I remember I tried to do the best I can to excel in class and most of my work weren't questionable • Most - not all - met with me and ask what I didn't understand and have me re-do assignments or explain their expectations again for future assignment • I wasn't doing well on literature essay and got F on this. The professor encouraged me to do better on this next time because literature is not my thing • Some of my professors expressed their concern or disappointment by asking me to meet with them after class and discuss about my lack of performance on homework's. Also discuss about their expectation of me in class. Mostly time I meet with my professors and asked for advice/feedback • I don't usually miss my homework unless it a reason. Usually my teacher understands the reason but did not care and make me miss homework • Most of my professor wait later when I am passing or failing • I made some mistakes and she followed up and showed me how to do better

Note. SQ = Survey Question; UG = Undergraduates participants; AL = Alumni participants

Table 30

Records: Behavior and Achievement

SQ	UG Responses (*n*=10)	AL Responses (*n*=10)
Provide an example of how professor's feedback discouraged you that led you to fail.	5 no feedback after grading 1 public discipline 1 low grade for hard work 1 get help no office hours 1 completely ignored 1 no answer	1 no feedback after grading 1 public discipline 2 low grades for hard work 1 public correction "wrong" 1 get help for unacceptable work but no office hours offered 4 no answer
How did your professor respond to you when you did not perform to his or her expectations?	4 positive verbal disappointments plus help after class 3 written disappointment on homework plus help after class 1 disappointment no follow up 1 cared about my education 1 not applicable	2 positive verbal disappointments plus help after class 2 written disappointment on homework plus help after class 3 disappointments, no follow up 2 cared about my education 1 body language and indifference

Note. SQ = Survey Question; UG = Undergraduates participants; AL = Alumni participants

Table 31

Consistent Treatment Participants

SQ	UG responses $n=10$	AL responses $n=10$
Give an example of how the professor's feedback encouraged you to succeed in the classroom.	The Professor gave me verbal and written feedback about my assignments	The Professor gave me verbal and written feedback about my assignments
	The Professor gave me verbal and written feedback about my assignments	The Professor gave me verbal and written feedback about my assignments
	The Professor gave me verbal and written feedback about my assignments	The Professor gave me verbal and written feedback about my assignments
	The Professor gave me verbal and written feedback about my assignments	The Professor gave me verbal and written feedback about my assignments
	The Professor gave me verbal and written feedback about my assignments	The Professor was consistent with feedback
	The Professor gave me verbal and written feedback about my assignments	The Professor was consistent with feedback
	The Professor was consistent with feedback	The Professor publicly gave me feedback about my work during team and individual activities
	The Professor publicly gave me feedback about my work during team and individual activities	The Professor publicly gave me feedback about my work during team and individual activities
	The Professor publicly cited my work as an example for others to follow	The Professor recommended my name for course-related panels and special events
	The Professor recommended my name for course-related panels and special events	The Professor recommended my name for course-related panels and special events

Note. SQ = Survey Question; UG = Undergraduates participants; AL = Alumni participants

Table 31a

Testimonies: Encouraged Feedback

SQ	UG Comments ($n=10$)	AL Comments ($n=10$)
Give an example of how the professor's feedback encouraged you to succeed in the classroom.	• These were always wow factors. When work was not up to par caused me to do better next time • I experienced this a few times. I was offered jobs and other leadership positions as well • Feedback is very necessary to access your progress in a class • Because help me to understand on feedback when I turned in for homework or project	• I cannot count how many times I was asked to be part of a panel related to a class I had recently taken. Many times it had to do with my being a person of color but I was somewhat okay with it. • One professor was particularly good at it. He challenged me with his meticulous criticism. • The consistency of the professor's feedback helped me to do well in classroom. • Both verbally and written throughout the class helps a lot • Cultural differences - acceptable feedback without insulting or conflict • That's the professor's continuation to see myself to be successes in classroom • Usually getting the feedback on the positive note, nothing about want to improve or want to work out. • But that's after I prove that I am academic success • She want me to success no matter what. Had very high expectation on me

Notes:

Table 32

Helpful Activities Participants

SQ	UG responses $n=10$	AL responses $n=10$
What class activities did the professor use to help you succeed in class?	The Professor put me on a team with my classmates to work on class assignments together and checked to make sure I participated	The Professor put me on a team with my classmates to work on class assignments together and checked to make sure I participated
	The Professor put me on a team with my classmates to work on class assignments together and checked to make sure I participated	The Professor put me on a team with my classmates to work on class assignments together and checked to make sure I participated
	The Professor put me on a team with my classmates to work on class assignments together and checked to make sure I participated	The Professor put me on a team with my classmates to work on class assignments together and checked to make sure I participated
	The Professor put me on a team with my classmates to work on class assignments together and checked to make sure I participated	The Professor put me on a team with my classmates to work on class assignments together and checked to make sure I participated
	The Professor put me on a team with my classmates to work on class assignments together and checked to make sure I participated	The Professor called upon me to answer questions and probed me for answers even when I didn't raise my hand
	The Professor put me on a team with my classmates to work on class assignments together and checked to make sure I participated	The Professor called upon me to answer questions and probed me for answers even when I didn't raise my hand
	The Professor called on me to help other classmates and gave us verbal praise even when we couldn't answer	The Professor called upon me to answer questions and probed me for answers even when I didn't raise my hand
	The Professor often asked me to solve problems on the blackboard, which was common for other classmates as well	The Professor often asked me to solve problems on the blackboard, which was common for other classmates as well
	The Professor maintained eye contact and smiled at me all the time in class when he or she probed for answers from me	The Professor gave pop quizzes to help us maintain good grades in class
	The Professor gave pop quizzes to help us maintain good grades in class	The Professor gave pop quizzes to help us maintain good grades in class

Note. SQ = Survey Question; UG = Undergraduates participants; AL = Alumni participants

Table 32a

Inquiries: Galatea Effects

SQ	UG Comments (*n*=10)	AL Comments (*n*=10)
What class activities did the professor use to help you succeed in class?	• This would bring the best out of me • I think what helped was the fact that my professors noticed the shyness that I have. They know what I am capable of but I hold myself back. Some of these professors have really helped me open up. • Leader! • It's good the measure where you can from time to time with a pop quiz • Specific what professor wants that will apply to the test or paper work to type • That's only was the professor was able to see if I'm being learned from the professor carefully in class. • As my major in graphic design I was require to work with the students to complete the project. It where it gave me a hard time to work with them because the don't have work ethic like I do. I have to do most of the work because it can affect my grade. • She always does that and we get extra credit for participated	• These quizzes determined how much information I was actually learning and remembering. Listening skills was better than I expected. • I got motivated when I have enough attention considering my extroverted personality • The professor called me to respond to questions when I didn't raise my hand. This tactics ensures that I read the assignment and familiarize myself with the content. • Professors does it equally for me and call students who doesn't participate • Presentation (PowerPoint) with specific topic good team building with peers

Note. SQ = Survey Question; UG = Undergraduates participants; AL = Alumni participants

Table 33

Performed Above Expectations Participants

SQ	UG responses $n=10$	AL responses $n=10$
How did your professor respond to you when you performed above expectations?	My Professor verbally gave me positive reinforcement and privately encouraged me to continue doing well	My Professor verbally gave me positive reinforcement and privately encouraged me to continue doing well
	My Professor verbally gave me positive reinforcement and privately encouraged me to continue doing well	My Professor verbally gave me positive reinforcement and privately encouraged me to continue doing well
	My Professor verbally gave me positive reinforcement and privately encouraged me to continue doing well	My Professor verbally gave me positive reinforcement and privately encouraged me to continue doing well
	My Professor verbally gave me positive reinforcement and privately encouraged me to continue doing well	My Professor verbally gave me positive reinforcement and privately encouraged me to continue doing well
	My Professor verbally gave me positive reinforcement and privately encouraged me to continue doing well	My Professor wrote positive comments on my paper
	My Professor wrote positive comments on my paper	My Professor wrote positive comments on my paper
	My Professor wrote positive comments on my paper	My Professor wrote positive comments on my paper
	My Professor wrote positive comments on my paper	My Professor wrote positive comments on my paper
	My Professor publicly praised my work in classroom and used me as an example to show his or her expectations	It was difficult to tell if my Professor was praising my work because he or she made general statements to the entire class
	It was difficult to tell if my Professor was praising my work because he or she made general statements to the entire class	It was difficult to tell if my Professor was praising my work because he or she made general statements to the entire class

Note. SQ = Survey Question; UG = Undergraduates participants; AL = Alumni participants

Table 33a

Accounts: Performed Above Expectations

SQ	UG Comments (*n*=10)	AL Comments (*n*=10)
How did your professor respond to you when you performed above expectations?	• They comment something if I do great • They would make sure I continued to do well without making others feel lesser • My professor would write profound statements on my papers if I did really well or surpassed her/his expectations • See me around, smile, and acting like he know me being successful easily • He was proud of me to do hard works in class • Because after while positive and know my weakness about homework	• In some of my papers my professor praised my work. At times when I needed feedback the most to assure I was in the right track my professors did this. • Simple as that! • While expectations were established in class, I don't recall being praised for my good work to the point where everyone in class would acknowledge it so it wasn't clear. • They would write comments on my paper like "good point" or "analysis" • When I complete the assignments, professors were impressed & gave me fair grades • Because it's only way to know professor is doing great of teaching which means I'm b/c I meet the expectations successfully if not then I'll fail the class. • Some teacher push me really hard to improve my work quality to succeed my level where I can produce in real world. Most teacher will just leave me alone as I am the best student in class that don't need any help and help other students more than me. • Not all but I have to compete with White folks/students to recognize my performance • When she saw my work, she always telling me to keep it up and she knew I can do it

Note. SQ = Survey Question; UG = Undergraduates participants; AL = Alumni participants

Table 34

Outperformed Classmates Participants

SQ	UG responses $n=10$	AL responses $n=10$
Describe an example of how your professor encouraged you to perform better than your classmates.	My Professor publicly gave me positive feedback about my work in class	My Professor publicly gave me positive feedback about my work in class
	My Professor publicly gave me positive feedback about my work in class	My Professor met with me frequently to help me clarify assignments
	My Professor publicly gave me positive feedback about my work in class	My Professor provided generic feedback to everyone in class
	My Professor publicly gave me positive feedback about my work in class	My Professor provided generic feedback to everyone in class
	My Professor publicly gave me positive feedback about my work in class	My Professor provided generic feedback to everyone in class
	My Professor met with me frequently to help me clarify assignments	My Professor provided generic feedback to everyone in class
	My Professor met with me frequently to help me clarify assignments	My Professor provided generic feedback to everyone in class
	My Professor provided generic feedback to everyone in class	I cared about my education and worked hard to perform well in all my classes and did not need the Professor's feedback
	My Professor provided generic feedback to everyone in class	I cared about my education and worked hard to perform well in all my classes and did not need the Professor's feedback
	I cared about my education and worked hard to perform well in all my classes and did not need the Professor's feedback	Other, please describe-

Note. SQ = Survey Question; UG = Undergraduates participants; AL = Alumni participants

Table 34a

Enquiries: Excelled Performance

SQ	UG Comments (*n*=10)	AL Comments (*n*=10)
Describe how your professor encouraged you to perform better than your classmates.	• They always giving me feedback to make I can get a better grade • My Professor gave me more homework for extra credit • Again to make sure I stayed on track • Never had a professor do that • Being fair to other people • Because he want me to do well in class • Encouragement from teachers are nice but self motivation is better • Because feedback is always helpful so I can do better next time	• At one point it became clear that my program expected more from me than the other students. She informed me in a meeting before that she wanted me to challenge myself to do more to get my A's and exceed the papers expectation. At first I was happy that someone outside myself cared so much about my performance but when I received a B- after doing extra work and another student got an A and didn't cover half of the material that I did it really aggravated me. • A couple of professors were good at it. • While everyone's work may very to some extent, most of my professors provided general comments to the entire class without reaching out to further praise those like me who did better. • Professors give feedback for everyone. And if struggling, make additional comments. • Professors were impressed & praised when I provided my contribution to share with peers in classroom. • It's just felt that professor don't have time to help the student individually. So therefore the professor would like to save the time by saying it all at once in the classroom. • I met with my professor when I wanted to perform better for myself and classmates as well. I am very competitive person always strive to be the best I can be. Few of my professor encouraged me to perform better then my classmate but I wasn't expecting them to do that because knowing as professor job is to make sure all students succeed their academic – most • Even though some student don't do well or can't keep up with the class course, teacher will show them and wait for them to catch up with the course that other student like me that was already done long time ago • Because she noticed I always work hard no matter what without giving up

Note. SQ = Survey Question; UG = Undergraduates participants; AL = Alumni participants

Table 35

Indicators: Consistent Treatment

SQ	UG Responses (*n*=10)	AL Responses (*n*=10)
Give an example of how the professor's feedback encouraged you to succeed in the classroom.	6 verbal/written feedback on assignments 1 consistent feedback 1 public feedback 1 work was cited as class example 1 recommended name for panels and special events	4 verbal/written feedback on assignments 2 consistent feedback 2 public feedback 2 recommended name for panels and special events
What class activities did the professor use to help you succeed in class?	6 assigned to team with a follow up to ensure participation 1 eye contact during probing 1 called on to help others 1 solve problems for all to learn 1 pop quizzes	4 assigned to team with a follow up to ensure participation 3 called to answer questions and probed 1 solve common problems on blackboard 1 pop quizzes
How did your professor respond to you when you performed above expectations?	5 privately offered positive reinforcements 3 positive comments on paper 1 public praise and used as an example to support expectations 1 unclear due to generalized statements to all	4 privately offered positive reinforcements 4 positive comments on paper 2 unclear due to generalized statements to all
Describe how your professor's encouraged you to perform better than your classmates.	5 publicly gave feedback 2 frequent meetings to clarify assignments 2 generic feedback to all 1 cared about own education	1 publicly gave feedback 1 frequent meetings to clarify assignments 5 generic feedback to all 2 cared about own education 1 other: private meetings with my program advisor

Note. SQ = Survey Question; UG = Undergraduates participants; AL = Alumni participants

Table 36

Conform to the SFP Participants

SQ	UG responses *n*=10	AL responses *n*=10
What class activities did the professor use to help you feel academically challenged?	The Professor put me on a team with my classmates to work on class assignments together and checked to make sure I participated	The Professor put me on a team with my classmates to work on class assignments together and checked to make sure I participated
	The Professor put me on a team with my classmates to work on class assignments together and checked to make sure I participated	The Professor put me on a team with my classmates to work on class assignments together and checked to make sure I participated
	The Professor put me on a team with my classmates to work on class assignments together and checked to make sure I participated	The Professor put me on a team with my classmates to work on class assignments together and checked to make sure I participated
	The Professor put me on a team with my classmates to work on class assignments together and checked to make sure I participated	The Professor put me on a team with my classmates to work on class assignments together and checked to make sure I participated
	The Professor put me on a team with my classmates to work on class assignments together and checked to make sure I participated	The Professor called upon me to answer questions and probed me for answers even when I didn't raise my hand
	The Professor put me on a team with my classmates to work on class assignments together and checked to make sure I participated	The Professor called upon me to answer questions and probed me for answers even when I didn't raise my hand
	The Professor called on me to help other classmates and gave us verbal praise even when we couldn't answer	The Professor called upon me to answer questions and probed me for answers even when I didn't raise my hand
	The Professor often asked me to solve problems on the blackboard, which was common for other classmates as well	The Professor often asked me to solve problems on the blackboard, which was common for other classmates as well
	The Professor maintained eye contact and smiled at me all the time in class when he or she probed for answers from me	The Professor gave pop quizzes to help us maintain good grades in class
	The Professor gave pop quizzes to help us maintain good grades in class	The Professor gave pop quizzes to help us maintain good grades in class

Note. SQ = Survey Question; UG = Undergraduates participants; AL = Alumni participants

Table 36a

Mentions: Academically Challenged

SQ	UG Comments (*n*=10)	AL Comments (*n*=10)
What class activities did the professor use to help you feel academically challenged?	• To remind me I can do this. Helped me slow down and focus. • This kept us on our toes. • Good feelings • He want to make sure that I participate a lot which he will give more credit • Helps to keep information fresh in your mind • Because the participated with classmate is key	• Professors always tended to want to know what I think first before any other students in the class. • It helps keeping the momentum on the roll • This tactics of calling me to respond to questions I didn't volunteer to answer helped prepare me to make sure I understand my reading materials before I come to class. • Feel just like another body. No expectations and making sure if I participated doesn't check to see if I understand the material • Some peers had different cultural backgrounds challenged me to accept & work better with peers that helped me fully aware in future jobs after graduation • That's only was the professor made sure I'll able to pass the course without any question asked. • It base on what type of course that I took. Some require my hard work because my teammate don't know how to make it work. Some I learned from my teammate than what I learn from my teachers. • She want to make sure I am paying attention and did my homework

Note. SQ = Survey Question; UG = Undergraduates participants; AL = Alumni participants

Table 37

Failed due to Expectations Participants

SQ	UG responses *n*=10	AL responses *n*=10
If applicable, provide an example showing that you failed academically because of your professor's expectations.	No answer	My Professor did not give me verbal praise in class about my academic performance
	My Professor and I did not discuss my performance	No answer
	My Professor and I did not discuss my performance	My Professor often shared discouraging words with me about my performance
	No answer	My Professor often shared discouraging words with me about my performance
		My Professor often shared discouraging words with me about my performance
	My Professor did not give me additional homework to help academic performance	No answer
	No answer	I cared about my education but my Professor didn't seem to care at all
	N/A	Other, please describe-
	My Professor often shared discouraging words with me about my performance	Other, please describe-
	Other, please describe-	Other, please describe-

Note. SQ = Survey Question; UG = Undergraduates participants; AL = Alumni participants

Table 37a

Inquests: Academic Failure due to Expectations

SQ	UG Comments (*n*=10)	AL Comments (*n*=10)
If applicable, provide an example showing that you failed academically because of your professor's expectations.	• Had one professor who was very apathetic. I went through some really tough times (death etc.) seems like she did not care • Because I admitted not feel like to meet	• Despite failing my only course ever my professor was highly critical of me the whole semester. Upon taking the course there was no change of her attitude but I didn't expect any since I made up my mind that I was going to do it for my own good & pass • I remember clearly one professor didn't really care for my academia except himself especially when I was in fatal accident that really cost my life. Instead, he said, "don't worry. I will just give you an F then you can come back to retake class to replace the grade," when there was only 2 weeks left before exam. I have noticed he wasn't really interested in empowering Black males. When ladies approached, he become more attentive. • Didn't set expectations and give vague feedback like "I see the potential in you" comments • One of my major professor happens to find lack of integrity in my academic coursework because it was very difficult for me to understand. And I wasn't asked to get more assignment to pull the grade up • Some of my professor - mostly White professor shared discouraging words with me by saying I won't pass their class if I continue to not doing well on my homework even though I hardly understand professors teaching. It was frustrated as I had set my goals to pass all my courses and get above 3.0 GPA. I didn't let my professors to slow me down I fought it through till the end. • When I am having low grades, she kept telling me to come to see her after class to make it better

Note. SQ = Survey Question; UG = Undergraduates participants; AL = Alumni participants

Table 38

Succeeded due to Expectations Participants

SQ	UG responses *n*=10	AL responses *n*=10
Describe an example showing that you succeeded academically because of your professor's expectations.	My Professor's reminders about expectations helped me succeed	My Professor's reminders about expectations helped me succeed
	My Professor's reminders about expectations helped me succeed	My Professor's reminders about expectations helped me succeed
	My Professor's one-on-one attention to my performance helped me succeed	My Professor's one-on-one attention to my performance helped me succeed
	My Professor's one-on-one attention to my performance helped me succeed	My Professor's one-on-one attention to my performance helped me succeed
	My Professor's one-on-one attention to my performance helped me succeed	My Professor's one-on-one attention to my performance helped me succeed
	My Professor's one-on-one attention to my performance helped me succeed	My Professor's verbal praise in class about my academic performance motivated me to succeed
	My Professor's verbal praise in class about my academic performance motivated me to succeed	I cared about my education and worked hard to perform well in all my classes and did not need the Professor's feedback
	My Professor provided encouraging words such as "Good job," or "Keep up the good work, I am proud of you."	I cared about my education and worked hard to perform well in all my classes and did not need the Professor's feedback
	My Professor provided encouraging words such as "Good job," or "Keep up the good work, I am proud of you."	I cared about my education and worked hard to perform well in all my classes and did not need the Professor's feedback
	My Professor provided encouraging words such as "Good job," or "Keep up the good work, I am proud of you."	I cared about my education and worked hard to perform well in all my classes and did not need the Professor's feedback

Note. SQ = Survey Question; UG = Undergraduates participants; AL = Alumni participants

Table 38a

Interpositions: Academic Success due to Expectations

SQ	UG Comments (*n*=10)	AL Comments (*n*=10)
Describe an example showing that you succeeded academically because of your professor's expectations.	• Sometimes this was done to motivate others to excel also • I was at a point where I could have given up but my teacher did not give up on me. I allowed my own personal issues to get in the way of my academic performance. She saw that and helped me focus on my work • One-on-one attention save my time • No comment • Kind words to let me know I'm on the right track • Because I like one on one that group. It caused me distraction. Best way to see professor during office hour or after class privately	• Failure was not an option for me. I didn't follow a programs expectation. I set them on my own. I did this because once those professors gone I have to exceed expectation for the rest of my life. So I set them for myself rather than depend on them. • I have an extroverted personality and receive energy from people to exceed people's expectations. For every class I received an A is one I frequently receive one-and-one attention from professor • I succeeded academically because of expectations I established for myself. I don't remember being able to credit my professor for my academic achievements because most of the times they weren't communicated directly to me. • Constant reminders to the students of one's expectations • "Good job," "Excellent" were very positive from professor • That's only way to pass the course in order to graduate from the university on the time. • I encouraged myself to meet one-on-one with my professor in order to get better understanding and improve my academic performance. • Teacher will expect me to pass the course without any trouble or issue. Sometime when felt like the course is easy where I can pass it flying color. I asked for exceed but never really make me don't I think it because it too much work for teacher to make • Basically I do it all on my own. • Because I always go to see her after class when I need her

Note. SQ = Survey Question; UG = Undergraduates participants; AL = Alumni participants

Table 39

Figures: SFP

SQ	UG Responses (*n*=10)	AL Responses (*n*=10)
What class activities did the professor use to help you feel academically challenged?	1 Not applicable 2 called on to answer plus probe 2 perform task on blackboard 1 eye contact probing for answers 1 Pop quizzes to maintain grades	3 called on to answer plus probe 1 assigned me to lead a group on special assignment 1 Pop quizzes to maintain grades
If applicable, provide an example showing that you failed academically because of your professor's expectations.	1 shared discouraging words 2 no additional homework 2 did not discuss performance 1 other: no effort 3 no answer	3 shared discouraging words 1 no verbal praise 1 cared about own education 3 other: N/A; she does care; no expectation with vague feedback 2 no answer
Describe an example showing that you succeeded academically because of your professor's expectations.	2 reminders 4 one-on-one attention 1 verbal praise 3 encouraging words - "good job"	2 reminders 3 one-on-one attention 1 verbal praise 4 cared about my own education

Note. SQ = Survey Question; UG = Undergraduates participants; AL = Alumni participants

More Books!

I want morebooks!

Buy your books fast and straightforward online - at one of the world's fastest growing online book stores! Environmentally sound due to Print-on-Demand technologies.

Buy your books online at
www.get-morebooks.com

Kaufen Sie Ihre Bücher schnell und unkompliziert online – auf einer der am schnellsten wachsenden Buchhandelsplattformen weltweit! Dank Print-On-Demand umwelt- und ressourcenschonend produziert.

Bücher schneller online kaufen
www.morebooks.de

OmniScriptum Marketing DEU GmbH
Heinrich-Böcking-Str. 6-8
D - 66121 Saarbrücken
Telefax: +49 681 93 81 567-9

info@omniscriptum.com
www.omniscriptum.com